CHINESE ART

by

LEIGH ASHTON
& BASIL GRAY

FABER AND FABER
24 Russell Square
London

First published in November Mcmxxxv
by Faber and Faber Limited
24 Russell Square London W.C. 1
Second impression January Mcmxxxvi
Third impression January Mcmxlv
Fourth impression January Mcmxlvii
Printed in Great Britain by
R. MacLehose and Company Limited
The University Press Glasgow

C C

PREFACE

We do not aim in this book at doing more than supply a very short introduction to the history of Chinese Art and a series of illustrations of each period of that history. Such is the long and complicated development of the various branches of the Arts which thrived in China, that it would not be possible in a hundred and forty plates to give anything but the briefest glimpse of a civilization which has so many sides, and our selection of those plates must therefore be arbitrary and leave many gaps. In the same way our introductory essay only skims the surface of the subject, though the notes to the plates contain more detailed supplementary information. But the arrangement of so many Western museums having been based on a principle of division by material, and the system of all books on Chinese Art written in English having hitherto followed that principle, we have thought it worth while to put together a sequence of illustrations by periods; for there can be no question but that the appreciation of the culture of a particular epoch depends, to a large extent, on the inter-relation of the various branches of Art, and their dependence on the intellectual and material standards of that epoch. It is easier, therefore, to get some insight into the importance of the particular period, with which one is concerned, by a small group of plates showing picked pieces of the highest quality in every branch of the Arts, than by having to pursue the thread of one's investigation through a series of chapters dealing with various materials. Our selection has been governed to a certain extent by the fact that there are no coloured plates in this book. The examples of Sung ceramics, for instance, have been chosen primarily with a view to their form, and it is for this reason that the *Tz'ŭ chou* wares are more strongly represented than their more aristocratic cousins the *Chün, Ko* or *Kuan yao*, while the most famous of all, *Ju yao*, does not appear at all. For the same reason we have reproduced very few jades and no example of eighteenth-century self-colour porcelain. The selection of the paintings and the accompanying notes are by Mr Basil Gray; of the remainder and their notes by Mr Leigh Ashton; in the introductory matter the same division holds good. The Wade system of transliteration is used through-out, but in the matter of the breathings, regarding which there is a certain divergence of practice, we have reverted to the use of the apos-trophe, laid down by Bushell in his *Chinese Art*. We are indebted to Professor Yukio Yashiro and Miss Margery Fry for obtaining photo-graphs from China and Japan, and the following for permission to repro-duce works of Art in their possession: The Chinese Government; the British Museum; the Victoria and Albert Museum; the Louvre; the Museum für Völkerkunde, Berlin; the National Museum and the Ostasia-

5

Preface

tiska Samlingarna, Stockholm; Röhsskakabinet, Göteborg; the Metro-
politan Museum, New York; the Museum of Fine Arts, Boston; the
University Museum of Philadelphia; the Freer Gallery of Art, Washing-
ton; the Museum of Fine Arts, Detroit; the William Rockwell Nelson
Gallery, Kansas City; the Marienkirche, Danzig; Sir Percival David, Bt;
Mr H. Oppenheim; Mrs Walter Sedgwick; Mrs Charles Rutherston;
Mr R. B. Bruce; Hon. and Mrs R. W. Bliss; Mr Raymond Bidwell; Mr
Greville L. Winthrop; Mr A. L. Peters; Mr and Mrs John D. Rockefel-
ler, Jr; M. Adolphe Stoclet; Dr F. von Klemperer; Herr F. Gutmann;
Mrs Wilfred Buckley; Mr Wright Ludington; M. Lagrelius.

CONTENTS

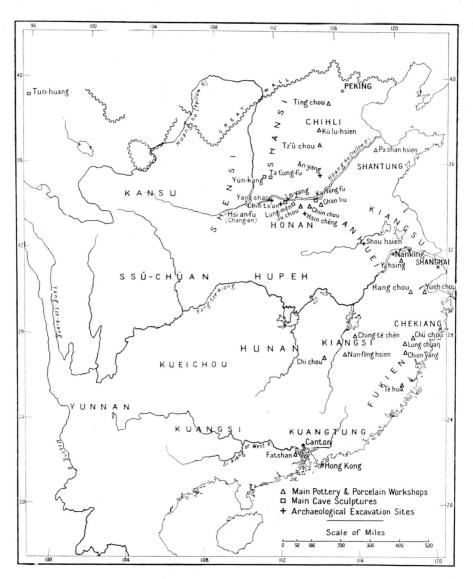

A Map of China
showing the main sites of archaeological excavation,
pottery and porcelain workshops, and cave sculptures

LIST OF PLATES

9

List of Plates

List of Plates

List of Plates

List of Plates

List of Plates

List of Plates

15

CHRONOLOGY OF CHINESE DYNASTIES AND PERIODS

SHANG-YIN	? 1766–1122 B.C.
CHOU	1122–249 B.C.
Period of the Spring and Autumn Annals	c. 722–481 B.C.
Period of the Warring States	c. 481–206 B.C.
CH'IN (Empire of Shih Huang Ti)	221–206 B.C.
EASTERN HAN	206 B.C.–25 A.D.
WESTERN HAN	25–220 A.D.
THE THREE KINGDOMS	220–280 A.D.
THE SIX DYNASTIES	220–589 A.D.
WESTERN AND EASTERN CHIN	265–419 A.D.
THE FIVE DYNASTIES	420–618 A.D.
PERIOD OF NORTHERN AND SOUTHERN DYNASTIES:	
Liu Sung ⎫	420–478 A.D.
Southern Ch'i ⎪	479–501 A.D.
Liang ⎬ South	502–556 A.D.
Ch'ēn ⎭	557–589 A.D.
Northern Wei ⎫	386–535 A.D.
Eastern Wei ⎪	534–550 A.D.
Western Wei ⎬ North	535–557 A.D.
Northern Ch'i ⎪	550–577 A.D.
Northern Chou ⎭	557–581 A.D.
SUI	581–618 A.D.
T'ANG	618–906 A.D.
THE FIVE DYNASTIES	907–960 A.D.
LIAO AND WESTERN LIAO	907–1201 A.D.
NÜ CHIN	1115–1234 A.D.
SUNG	960–1279 A.D.
Northern Sung	960–1127 A.D.
Southern Sung	1127–1279 A.D.
YÜAN	1280–1368 A.D.
MING	1368–1644 A.D.
Hung Wu	1368–1398 A.D.
Chien Wēn	1399–1402 A.D.
Yung Lo	1403–1424 A.D.
Hung Hsi	1425 A.D.
Hsuan Tē	1426–1435 A.D.
Chēng T'ung	1436–1449 A.D.
Ching T'ai	1450–1457 A.D.
T'ien Shun	1457–1464 A.D.

Ch'ēng Hua	1465–1487 A.D.
Hung Chih	1488–1505 A.D.
Chēng Tē	1506–1521 A.D.
Chia Ching	1522–1566 A.D.
Lung Ch'ing	1567–1572 A.D.
Wan Li	1573–1620 A.D.
T'ien Ch'i	1621–1627 A.D.
Ch'ung Chēng	1628–1644 A.D.
CH'ING	1644–1912 A.D.
Shun Chih	1644–1661 A.D.
K'ang Hsi	1662–1722 A.D.
Yung Chēng	1723–1735 A.D.
Ch'ien Lung	1736–1795 A.D.
Chia Ch'ing	1796–1821 A.D.
Tao Kuang	1821–1850 A.D.
Hsien Fēng	1851–1861 A.D.
T'ung Chih	1862–1873 A.D.
Kuang Hsü	1874–1908 A.D.
Hsüan T'ung	1909–1912 A.D.

PRE-HAN DYNASTIES AND PERIODS

SHANG-YIN   ? 1766–1122 B.C.

CHOU   1122–249 B.C.

  Period of the Spring and Autumn Annals c. 722–481 B.C.

  Period of the Warring States   c. 481–206 B.C.

CH'IN (Empire of Shih Huang Ti)   221–206 B.C.

PRE-HAN PERIOD

(c. 3000 B.C.–206 B.C.)

NEOLITHIC POTTERY

We do not know at what period the Chinese race, as we know it, first made its appearance, but somewhere about the beginning of the third millennium B.C. a culture with pottery of a highly decorative character was in existence in the valley of the Yellow River, and it seems likely that the members of this culture were related on physiological grounds to the historical Chinese. This pottery, which is the chief aesthetic production of the race, has distinct affinities with that of other cultures from further west, notably those of Anau on the Russo-Persian border and Tripolje near Kiev. It is not at present possible to say if the type originated in one locality, rather than in another, and we must be content to accept its presence in several centres in Asia and to realize that of them all the Chinese branch provides the finest examples both from an aesthetic and from a technical point of view. The two chief sites in China are Ch'i ch'ia p'ing in Kansu and Yang shao ts'un in Honan, from the latter of which the most beautiful pieces have been recovered (*Pl.* 1*a*). The ware, of a fine-grained red-dish-buff material, is painted with strong rhythmical patterns of a geometric nature. In the Kansu specimens these patterns are in restrained and simple forms; in the Honan group elaborated with hatchings, and the interposition of rings and ellipses, while the colour, in both groups of black or purple, is varied in a more sophisticated manner. It seems likely, therefore, that the Honan site represents a somewhat later date of culture than that of Kansu. It is impossible not to recognize the affinity between the feeling underlying these patterns and that underlying Mycenaean art (*Pl.* 1*b*), but the similarity is hardly more than that between Peruvian tapestry ornament and the nomadic carpets of the Turcoman tribes and it would be unwise to draw any conclusions. While there seems reason to suppose that the people who made this pottery were Chinese in appearance, there has been discovered at present nothing which links up in any satisfactory way their culture with that of historic China proper; this may be said to start approximately about the sixteenth century B.C.

EARLY HISTORIC CHINA

There is nothing primitive about the beginnings of historic China; but as regards its art it is an age of elaborate and formal patterns, and the repertory of its culture is a bronze one. It may be suggested that the foundations of the Chinese bronze culture were worked out in some Central Asian valley and that climatic conditions pushed the people concerned eastward, perhaps through Yunnan, to diverge in two waves, one to the Yellow River and down it, and one to the Yang tze-kiang.

A number of inscribed bones have been recovered from the site of Hsiao t'un in Northern Honan, the capital during the Shang-yin period (eighteenth-twelfth century B.C.). From these writings we are able to tell that this early China was a barbaric country controlled by a savage feudal system far surpassing in its cruelty that of the Middle Ages. This feudal system continued throughout the succeeding Chou Dynasty and at no time was there any centralized government ruling the whole country. Consequently it must always be remembered that we know nothing of what differences in artistic style prevailed in different parts of the country, and almost all discussions must, in the present state of our information, rank as generalizations. A few simple cooking vessels in pottery foreshadow the forms of some types of bronzes of a later date, and some fragments of a finer pottery of white colour show simple types of geometric pattern, which once again are the forerunners and perhaps the inspirers of their bronze descendants. For it is with the large series of decorated vessels in bronze that Chinese Art first makes an important appearance, and, at present, it is difficult to place these with any certainty at an earlier date than about the twelfth century B.C., to which date we may approximately assign the important group found at An-yang in Northern Honan.

BRONZES

Bronzes, in some ways the most characteristic of all the forms of early Chinese Art, were made during the longest period of their use for ritual purposes, but derived their origin from the simple and domestic forms of everyday utensils; they may be divided roughly into five groups.

(*a*) Cooking and serving vessels of which the most important were the *ting*, a tripod vessel with a circular body, the *li*, also three-footed but with the feet hollow and forming part of the body, the *tui*, a four-handled, wide-mouthed cauldron, and the *fu*, an oblong rectangular trough on feet.

(*b*) Drinking and storing vessels, of which the most important were the *hu* (*Pl.* 9), a term for almost any tall vase with a wide body and small aperture, the *yu*, a covered vessel with a swing handle, the *chüeh*, a wine-cup on three feet, with handle and two projecting knobs on the rim, the *tsun* (*Pl.* 5*a*), a tall wine-beaker with flaring mouth and a wide knob in the middle, and the *ku*, a more elegant variety of the *tsun*.

(*c*) Vessels of a simpler domestic nature such as the *yi*, a wine-vessel in shape like a sauce-boat.

(*d*) Musical instruments such as the *chung* or bell, and the *ku* or drum.

(e) Weapons, such as the *ko*, a kind of halberd.

The decoration on the bronzes of the An-yang group consist as a rule of a ground-work of meander-like pattern known either as *lei wan* (thunder pattern) or *hui* (the Chinese character for revolving), on which appear *t'ao t'ieh* (a mythical monster) masks or *kuei* (conventionalized dragons), or other motives such as the cicada and the phoenix (*Pl. 2a*). As might be expected in a culture as primitive as this, these animal forms are treated in a particularly ferocious manner.

CHOU DYNASTY

With the Chou Dynasty (*c.* 1122–249 B.C.) the patterns undergo a change. In the earlier part of the period they seem to run riot in a medley of animal forms, which are frequently naturalistic as well as stylized, in both a departure from the previous style. In addition the number of kinds of animals is largely increased, while the human form occasionally appears. Legs and heads of animals are also used as decorative motives, while the bodies of the beasts are covered with patterns (*Pl. 5b*). At the edges of vessels appear serrated ridges and these ridges are often decorated with a series of hooks. The form of the various vessels remains strong.

In the latter part of the dynasty this exuberance of decoration is considerably reduced and horizontal bands of pattern alternating with plain surfaces seem to express a harmony of form and decoration arrived at after a period of stress (*Pl. 6*). The forms themselves show a more perfect proportion and in detail of handle or flare of mouth display a greater elegance than before. In all these early bronzes there is no question of inlay in precious metal though in the Shang-yin period a number of pieces with turquoise inlay are found, but time has added such beauties of patina to the metal that it needs no other ornament. Lovely greens, reds and blues are a feature of early Chinese bronze patination and certainly bronze in no other part of the world seems to find such means of adding to its natural beauty. In China this patina is sedulously ground down and polished, in Europe the natural incrustation is preferred.

EARLY JADES

In association with these early bronzes the archaic jades form a sister branch of early Chinese art. The beauties of jade were regarded in Ancient China as of supreme importance, both in ceremonial rites of religious intent and also in the smooth running of official and domestic life. Prescribed shapes and colours for use and for wear were essential in the endeavour to reconcile the opposing elements of the *yang* and the *ying*, the symbols of the positive male and the negative female principle of life. While most of them are simpler in character, as befits a material which depends for its value on play of colour and quality of surface, these jades display the same strength of form and effortless success in decoration as their bronze cousins. Their dating is a much more hazardous problem, but a number of them must be assigned to very early times, more notably perhaps the plain blades and axe-heads. The colour of these ritual jades varies from a creamy-white through every shade of buff and brown to greys, dark green and sometimes black. Their beauty of marking with its veins and splashes of varying tone is often emphasized by some slight decoration which breaks the light and shows off form and colour alike. The six ritual shapes are:

(*a*) the *pi*, a flat ring with a hole in the centre, which was used in the worship of heaven (*Pl.* 4*b*). The decoration on these disks, sometimes of grain forms, seems also to connect them with the festivals of the sowing or the harvest. Sky blue was the ceremonial colour.

(*b*) The *ts'ung*, a hollow cylinder in the form of a square enclosing a circle, symbolizing the earth (*Pl.* 4*a*). Yellow was the ceremonial colour.

(*c*) The *kuei*, a plaque in shape like a spear-head, used for worship to the East; its ceremonial colour was green.

(*d*) The *chang*, in shape like half a *pi*, used for worship to the South; its ceremonial colour was red.

(*e*) The *hu*, probably a plaque in the form of, or with the representation of a tiger on it, used for worship to the West; its ceremonial colour was white.

(*f*) The *huang*, a plaque in the form of a segment of a circle, used in worship to the North; its ceremonial colour was black.

Other forms frequently met with are axe-heads (*Pl.* 13*b*), knives (*Pl.* 3*a*), and smaller plaques in the form of animals (*Pl.* 8), some of which seem to have been used as tallies, others of which were employed in the elaborate ceremonies of the dressing of a corpse.

CONFUCIANISM

It was during the final stages of the Chou dynasty that was born in 551 B.C. China's most celebrated son, the philosopher Confucius. He passed the early part of his life visiting the various courts of China and endeavouring to convert them to his beliefs, but it was not till he settled in the Kingdom of Wei that he was enabled to perfect his system and institute it; this he accomplished in 495 B.C. Confucius did not institute a religion, he formed a code. This code is based to a certain extent on the early Chinese rites, the ceremonials of which were prescribed and legalized for the first time in the Chou dynasty. And it is these prescribed ceremonials that form the basis of all the Chinese love of 'antique tradition', so important in the history of their art. Ever since the remote ages the rites for family and tribal gatherings had been formulating themselves. Founded on the devotion of the people for their rulers, upon the respect of the young for their elders, the Chinese state has built up for itself a rigid tradition, which has lasted to the present day. In the same manner the forms of the ritual vessels have developed, and the 'antique tradition' has handed them on from generation to generation.

It is this ceremonial observance that underlies Confucius' great philosophy; a philosophy as sound and practical as it is remote from the supernatural. For Confucius' influence was directed to everyday problems, on the principle that man must set his earthly house in order lest he have no time for considering the problems of life and death. By his own personal life and sayings the sage turned men's thoughts to a sober and rational view of these mysteries, which is unusual, when one considers the age in which he lived. For Confucius was an agnostic: 'When life on earth is so difficult, how can we understand aught of the supernatural?' was one of his sayings. At a time when morals and customs had lapsed into freedom and licence Confucius inculcated a severe and rigid doctrine, the practical application and development of which was to form the background of a system of government that has lasted 2,500 years.

TAOISM

Almost at the same time was born in the state of Ch'u, another man almost as important in Chinese history, Lao-tzŭ, the exponent of the doctrine of Taoism. The doctrine that he preached is directly in opposition to that of Confucius, being a mystic philosophy of Nature. 'Tao', which means 'the way', is in one aspect the primordial power from which all things in nature have their being; this power later was personified as a divinity in T'ien tsun, the Lord of Heaven. Lao-tzŭ's mystic philosophy rapidly degenerated into a widespread code of magical practices and superstitions, and it was in this interpretation of its tenets that its great popularity lay. But at the same time it has always provided a rallying point for the liberal poet and thinker and inspired much that is best in Chinese painting. Taoism and Confucianism unite in one thing, in upholding the great domestic cult, the worship of the Ancestors.

PERIOD OF 'THE WARRING STATES'

Towards the end of the sixth century B.C. the Chou Empire began to be split up into various small states and a period of trouble set in known as 'the Warring States' (481–206 B.C.). It was at the close of this period that there appeared the celebrated Shih Huang Ti, ruler of the state of Ch'in, who welded all the factions into one empire and ruled as Emperor of all China from 221–206 B.C. He established a military state, destroyed the Confucian books, abolished feudalism and left a monument to himself for all time, the Great Wall of China (*Pl.* 11*b*), built at a sacrifice of we do not know how many lives to keep the barbarian marauders out of the country. When he died the country relapsed into disorder for a few years, but he had laid the foundations of the Chinese Empire.

The style of art, which succeeded that of the Chou dynasty, used to be referred to as Ch'in, and in more recent years as Huai style from the number of objects of the date found in the Huai valley, but it would seem more convenient to give it a dynastic name and the period of the Warring States is possibly a more suitable one, so long as it is remembered that the style was coming into being probably about seventy or eighty years before 481 B.C., the date at which that period commences. The severe tradition of form and decoration began to break down and a baroque but elegant type of pattern took its place. While forms become more refined and feminine, the decoration is more intricate and delicate (*Pl.* 9). Ground-work of interlaced spirals, complicated hooked and dot patterns, coiled dragons and phoenixes, elongated animal forms set against diaper grounds, and such motives as strings and plaits are executed with a control of design and a precision of technique which is outstanding. Elements of the so-called animal style from Central Asia, with its vivid decorative quality founded on naturalistic form, creep in, while towards the end of the period begin to appear some of the elaborately inlaid gold and silver pieces, which form such a characteristic branch of the art of the Han period (206 B.C.–220 A.D.); these formulae are present not merely in the larger pieces, but also in the smaller. It is at this date that begins the production of the long series of mirrors which lasted down to Sung times (960–1279 A.D.) and later. The 'Warring States' style is particularly happy in its decoration of the circle of the mirror-back, filling the ground with intricate small-scale patterns or posing contrasting motives in plain relief against them (*Pl.* 10).

THE LO-YANG FIND

It is impossible to leave the period of the Warring States without a mention of a question which has threatened to affect the whole chronology of bronzes. In 1929 began to appear a very large number of bronzes from tombs in Lo-yang, a large proportion of which were acquired by Bishop J. C. White for the Toronto Museum. Bishop White assumes that all the pieces he acquired came from the same group of tombs, and, on the evidence of the inscription on a set of bells known as the *Piao* bells, that all these objects are of the same date. The date of these bells is generally accepted as 550 B.C., and cannot in any case be later than 380 B.C. But it is difficult to believe that all the objects came from the same tomb or that all the tombs were of the same date, or indeed that all the objects came from the group of tombs from which Bishop White thought they did. The presence of a large quantity of bronzes inlaid with gold, of a group previously assumed to be Han, and the variety of the types seem to make it impossible to accept this. But one piece of supreme importance appeared among this mixture of pieces, a bowl with bands of ornament combining the style of the Warring States and the inlaid style of the Han period. Now while there is little difficulty in assuming that this is a transitional piece, it is at present impossible to accept the consequent redistribution of styles, which the assumption of the truth of all Bishop White's statements would involve. The majority of the pieces he found would seem to belong to the end of the period of the Warring States or the beginning of the Han dynasty; a certain num-ber are probably rather earlier; a few, such as the set of bells, may date even from the later Chou period. And what more likely than that there should be placed in a tomb in addition to the contemporary objects some cherished piece of venerable age?

I*a*. VASE
Yang-shao culture ; about 3000 B.C.

Pottery : Height 14"

OSTASIATISKA SAMLINGARNA, STOCKHOLM

Decorated with spiral forms in black and purple.

I*b*. VASE
Perhaps 3rd–2nd Millennium B.C.

Unglazed grey earthenware : Height 10"

BRITISH MUSEUM, LONDON

This extraordinary vessel stands by itself in early Chinese art. In type of body it is close in colouring and material to certain plainly decorated food vessels of the Chou period and earlier, but is unrelated to them in shape and decoration. The handles with their simple curve proceeding directly from the lip to the body of the vessel can only be paralleled in Chinese art in the earliest vessels of Andersson's Yang-shao find.

2*a*. CASKET (I)
Yin style : before 11th century B.C.

Bronze : Height 9″

MRS WALTER SEDGWICK, LONDON

This square, house-like vessel is a typical example of the most primitive style of bronze decoration we yet know, with fiercely expressed animal motives on a ground of pattern formerly known as thunder pattern (*lei wan*), but now called *hui*—from the Chinese term for revolving. The serrated ridges at the sides are very early examples of a type much used at a rather later date for breaking up the continuity of the patterns.
Probably from An-yang, the capital of the Yin state.

2*b*. AXE-HEAD
Yin style : before 11th century B.C.

Bronze : Width 6·8″

MR H. OPPENHEIM, LONDON

A ceremonial axe with decoration in the form of a *t'ao t'ieh* mask. The *t'ao t'ieh*, perhaps the commonest of all decorative motives on early Chinese bronzes, varies in type from the savage monster-head here shown to a comparatively tame-looking animal of a tiger-like appearance.
Probably from An-yang.

3*a*. CEREMONIAL HALBERD BLADE
Probably before 1000 B.C.

Buff jade : Length 6·75"

MR H. OPPENHEIM, LONDON

3*b*. HANDLE
An-yang style, c. 1100 B.C.

Jade : Height 5"

MR H. OPPENHEIM, LONDON

Whitish-brown jade, the pattern a phoenix with scrolling cloud-forms showing traces of red pigment.

The majority of early Chinese jades depend for their aesthetic value upon their subtle gradations of colour and surface quality added to their simple form and restrained decoration. To some people early jades seem merely archaeological, but it is difficult for anyone who has handled a first-rate jade to deny the exquisite use of material and a sense of form, which many sculptures lack.

4*a*. TS'UNG
Chou Dynasty

Jade : Height 4″

MR H. OPPENHEIM, LONDON

Greenish-brown jade. The form represents the earth and is decorated with strap-work of trigrams symbolizing the earth and the heavens. The *ts'ung* was used in the primary ritual of earth-worship and was probably also associated with fertility rites.

4*b*. JADE DISK (PI)
Chou Dynasty

Brownish-grey with white markings : Diameter 5″

BRITISH MUSEUM, LONDON (EUMORFOPOULOS COLLECTION)

An early example of the *pi*, the first of the prescribed objects in Chou times for ceremonial use.

Pre-Han Period

5a. BRONZE VESSEL (TSUN)

So-called Yin-chou style; about 11th–9th century B.C.

Reddish-green patina : Height 9"

CHARLES L. RUTHERSTON COLLECTION, ENGLAND

Decorated with *hui* (revolving) patterns and conventional *kuei* dragons.

5b. BRONZE VESSEL IN THE FORM OF AN ELEPHANT

So-called Yin-chou style; about 11th–9th century B.C.

Olive-green patina : Height 14"

LOUVRE, PARIS (CAMONDO COLLECTION)

6. BRONZE VESSEL (YU)
So-called Yin-chou style ; about 11th–9th century B.C.

Olive-green patina : Height 11″

VICTORIA AND ALBERT MUSEUM, LONDON
(EUMORFOPOULOS COLLECTION)

Decorated with bands of *hui* (revolving) patterns with *kuei* dragons and
t'ao t'ieh masks.

7. POLE-END
Middle Chou style ; c. 9th–6th century B.C.

Bronze : Height 13·5″

WILLIAM ROCKHILL NELSON GALLERY OF ART,
KANSAS CITY, U.S.A.

8*a*. BUFFALO
Chou Dynasty (1122–249 B.C.)

Jade : Width 2″

Whitish-buff jade with traces of red pigment.

MR H. OPPENHEIM, LONDON

8*b*. OWL
Chou Dynasty (1122–249 B.C.) or earlier

Matrix of Turquoise

MRS WALTER SEDGWICK, LONDON

8*c*. OWL
Chou Dynasty (1122–249 B.C.) or earlier

Jade

MRS WALTER SEDGWICK, LONDON

Pale buff jade.

8*d*. FISH
Chou Dynasty (1122–249 B.C.)

Jade : Length 5″

MR H. OPPENHEIM, LONDON

Glaucous green jade.

9. BRONZE VESSEL (HU)
Period of Warring States (481–206 B.C.)

Bronze : Height 14″

VICTORIA AND ALBERT MUSEUM, LONDON
(EUMORFOPOULOS COLLECTION)

Both this and the mirror-back (*Pl.* 10) are typical examples of the somewhat restless, complicated style of pattern which succeeded the vigorous designs of the Chou dynasty. The more elegant forms, the appearance of the so-called 'Animal style' of Central Asia, the use of extreme detail are features of a period which has in it a distinctly baroque element.

IO. MIRROR-BACK
Period of Warring States (481–206 B.C.)

Bronze : Diameter 5″

OSTASIATISKA SAMLINGARNA, STOCKHOLM

This mirror-back with its design of elongated dragons on a diaper ground is an outstanding example of the elegant style of the Warring States.

IIa. STONE DRUMS FROM THE CONFUCIAN TEMPLE, PEKING
Chou Dynasty (1122–249 B.C.)

Height : about 3 ft.

These celebrated relics of Chinese antiquity were dug up in the early part of the seventh century A.D. and have been venerated ever since. The inscriptions consist of odes in honour of an Imperial hunting and fishing party, at which various feudal princes were present.

IIb. THE GREAT WALL
3rd century B.C.

Built by Shih Huang Ti as a protection against the Hsiung-nu barbarian horsemen.

HAN DYNASTY PERIODS

EASTERN HAN	206 B.C.–25 A.D.
WESTERN HAN	25–220 A.D.

HAN DYNASTY
(206 B.C.–220 A.D.)

The confusion into which China fell with the death of the dictator Shih Huang Ti did not last long. The house of Han assumed power and from 206 B.C.–220 A.D. ruled a kingdom, which by means of a far-sighted internal and foreign policy expanded into a wide and important Empire. The Han rulers succeeded in that most difficult task, the combination after a dictatorship of the best elements of an autocracy with the more moderate views of a representative government. Abroad, the foreign expeditions of the great Emperor Wu Ti (140–87 B.C.) and later the campaigns of the great General Pan Ch'ao (73–97 A.D.) carried the limits of the Empire to India and Persia and contact was made with the Roman Empire. At home, in the consequent expansion of trade the rich and peaceful position of the Central part of the Empire was conducive to the development of the Arts.

BRONZES

Bronze is still of great importance. The somewhat restless elegance of the Warring States style gives way to a simple and severe art. While in form the vessels are closely related to those of the latter part of the Warring States period, a still further refinement weakens the strength of the shapes, while ridges and sharply-defined rims add sophistication to the elegant lines (*Pl.* 14). Inlay of the most elaborate description in precious metals (*Pl.* 12), turquoise (*Pl.* 15a) or malachite, and gilding and silvering of the surface (*Pl.* 15b), are new features, while the most characteristic difference in the style is the extensive use of naturalistic animal and human forms.

ANIMAL STYLE

The treatment of these animal motives is one of the most marked elements of Han art and one of its most important. A tendency to elongate the forms (*Pl.* 13b), a tendency no doubt derived from the West—such forms are common enough in Graeco-Bactrian art and probably represent an Iranian element—gives an effect of suppressed nervous energy and an enhanced feeling for movement. This feeling is emphasized by the frequent use of a formula often known as the 'flying gallop' (*Pl.* 52a), by which an animal in movement is shown with all four feet outstretched, a position it does not use in nature. Both in bronze and jade we have many examples of this light and attractive use of animal forms, in none more than in the series of fibulae (*Pl.* 15), which are one of the most characteristic groups of the smaller examples of applied art. These belt or cloak-hooks are either openwork in the form of dragons or some

49

other slender animal, or solid with inlay or relief work of similar design; the hook is usually formed as an animal head while some of the decoration contains clearly planned geometric motives, the most frequent patterns comprising combinations of triangles, ovals and spirals.

The mirror-backs at this date are also of great beauty and variety (*Pl.* 25*a*). The majority are decorated in concentric zones round a central boss to contain the cord by which the mirror was held. Various types of design are the 'hundred nipples' with a series of cones, in reality representing stars; the 'eight bows', a circular motive divided by eight segmentary arcs; the 'swallows' wings', a geometrical arrangement with radiating wing-like motives; and there are many others.

POTTERY

It is in this epoch that there appears the first glazed pottery of importance, though it is just possible that some roughly-glazed ware existed considerably earlier.[1] It is not known whether the Chinese invented this glaze or imported it as the result of contact with more Western States, but certainly the most typical colour, a rich dark green (*Pl.* 20), closely resembles that found on certain Roman and Parthian pottery. Most of the Han pottery we possess has been recovered from tombs; for it has always been the custom of the Chinese to bury with their dead series of models of objects for domestic use and pleasure, which the dead man might be expected to need in his future life. It is the survival of the custom, which in earlier times demanded the sacrifice of wives, servants, and animals at the funeral ceremony.

Many of the pieces are plain, but others, more especially those which imitate metal forms, have elaborate designs in relief. In particular a class of vase with modelled hunting scenes round the shoulder forms one of the most important groups of artistic interest of these early times.

The typical body of Han pottery is of a soft brick-red material; the glazes are derived from lead, which is as a rule stained with copper oxide to give it a green colour. Through burial most of the Han pottery shows decomposition which has given the surface a gold or silver iridescence. In certain cases the pottery is unglazed and is of a dark grey colour. The finest examples of this group are decorated with freely drawn designs in unfired pigment, usually red and white (*Pl.* 21*a*). In this grey material there exist also a number of tiles with lively animal designs either incised or in relief; these latter have a marked sculptural quality.

[1] An important glazed vessel in the William Rockwell Kent gallery of Art, Kansas City, may be dated with certainty in the period of the Warring States by reason of its decoration.

Han Dynasty

And the Han dynasty is the first period from which we possess a considerable quantity of sculptural material. Of this the most characteristic is the series of bas-reliefs found in tombs (*Pl.* 16). The main group of these reliefs is to be found in the Wu Liang tombs in Shantung and consists of two series dated 129 A.D. and 147–149 A.D. It is generally accepted that these reliefs are based on paintings, probably on historical frescoes such as existed in the Ling-Kuang palace of that date. Some of these carvings with simple incised scenes follow the painter's inspiration more closely than those in which the figures are cut in flat relief and polished, while the background is left in the rough stone. There is a simplicity about these Han reliefs which is attractive. Treated in a purely linear manner the outline is strongly drawn, while the rhythm and movement of the long bands of figures is well controlled and varies sufficiently to sustain the interest. Certain conventions such as the showing of rank by alteration in size point to a workshop of somewhat prescribed formula, but within these limits the designer achieved an individuality which is astonishing.

Apart from these reliefs there are a number of pieces of sculpture in the round. On the pillars of Ch'en at Chü hsien in Ss'ŭ-chüan, a series of carvings in deep relief of hunting-scenes and animal subjects (*Pl.* 17) are carved with a robust vigour, which shows not merely a highly developed sense of decoration, but also considerable ideas as to the adaptation of decoration to architectural needs. This sculpture is much more successful than the few pieces in the full round still in existence. The most important of these is the group of a horse trampling on a barbarian in front of the tomb of General Ho Ch'ü-ping, one of Wu Ti's generals in his campaign against the West, who died in 119 B.C. In some of the smaller pieces, notably among the earthenware figurines (*ming ch'i*) found in the tombs, there begins to appear that lively sense of naturalistic representation (*Pl.* 21*b*), which comes to its fullest flower under the T'ang dynasty (618–906 A.D.). Side by side with this naturalism appears an extreme of stylism, notably in small jade figures, where a man is reduced to three triangles, a pig to a cylinder, with a few deft strokes marking the form (*Pl.* 18*b*). These extremes meet in a few masterpieces such as the jade head of a horse in the Victoria and Albert Museum (*Pl.* 27).

PAINTING

We know that painting was widely practised under the Han dynasty and can gain some idea of the vanished wall-paintings in the Han palaces from the bas-reliefs which have already been mentioned. It is an art devoted to the service of the state just as was the art of Sasanian Persia or Imperial Rome. The virile stylization of men and animals in highly compact forms is evidence of advanced sophistication without a trace of decadence. Han art may not be so well calculated to impress as that of Rome or Persia, but it is the product of a people with greater sensibility. This is borne out by the fragments of actual painting that survive. At Boston, in the British Museum, and in Japan are now to be seen painted bricks recovered from tombs of the second or early third century A.D., which were opened during the construction of railways in Northern China. The bricks at Boston, which are the best preserved, show courtiers, men and women, watching an animal fight staged in the Imperial garden (*Pl.* 24). The British Museum fragments, which are probably earlier in date, are Taoist in character, and show the spirits of the dead borne to the other world in heavenly cars (*Pl.* 22). Both are summary and not monumental paintings, but they give an idea of the artist's personal attitude to his subject and of the range of their art. The Taoist picture, behind which lies a faith in magic and belief in occult powers, which are characteristic of the Taoist revival in the second century A.D., succeeds in conveying a rare sense of cosmic space and supernatural speed, while the secular painting, though it does not quite succeed in the attempt to express a social relationship between the figures represented, is more skilful, more vigorous and more graceful in drawing.

TEXTILES

The labours of Sir Aurel Stein in 1914 on the overland route from China to the Near East and those of the Kozloff Expedition in 1924–25 in the region of Lake Baikal brought to light a number of fragments of figured silk (*Pl.* 18a, 19b). The patterns are of a complicated nature, with the typical elongated animal-forms of Han design and cloud scrolls, strong swirling lines and neat diapers. But in these silks, the skill of technique and the control of the elaborate designs show plainly that a long history of textile development lies behind these consummate achievements. It is known that the Romans used Chinese silks and it is clear that the export trade in this commodity must have been considerable. It seems therefore likely that even at this period, as they did at later dates, the Chinese weavers were making, in addition to the goods for the native market, export products for other countries, and it is likely that some of these pieces still exist in European treasuries, their Chinese origin unrecognized.

Han Dynasty

The similarity of design prevailing in all branches of the applied arts is well shown by a few pieces of lacquer (*Pl. 19a*), which have survived from this early time. Here the same strong sense of linear pattern persists as on the bronzes and textiles and it is as the exponent of the best in applied art that Han design reaches its highest point.

12. DISK

Han Dynasty (206 B.C.–220 A.D.), or earlier

Bronze, inlaid with gold and silver : Diameter 6·5"

HON. ROBERT AND MRS WOODS BLISS, WASHINGTON

This marvellous disk forms part of the same find as the bull's head (cf. Pl. 13*a*). Considerations of date are discussed with that piece, and it is sufficient to add that this is a masterpiece of design.

13*a*. AXLE-CAP

Probably Han Dynasty (206 B.C.–220 A.D.)
Bronze inlaid with gold and silver, from Chin-ts'un, near Lo-yang, Honan

Length 6·5″

BRITISH MUSEUM, LONDON

This type of inlaid bronze is most commonly associated with the Han dynasty: but among the other objects found at the same time as this bull's head was a bronze bell which by its historical inscription can be assigned to a date in the sixth century B.C., and this piece therefore has been given to that date by some authorities. There does not seem at present sufficient reason to accept this early dating for the whole of the Chin-ts'un find.

13*b*. CEREMONIAL AXE-HEAD

Han Dynasty (206 B.C.–220 A.D.)

Jade : Width 6″

BRITISH MUSEUM, LONDON (EUMORFOPOULOS
COLLECTION)

The axe-head of greenish-yellow jade, suffused with warm brown passages, is remarkable for the superb animal composition of the handle. The dragon with the rabbit on its back is an admirable example of the elongation of animal form characteristic of the Han dynasty.

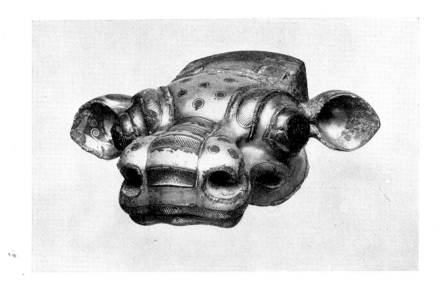

14. BRONZE VESSEL (HU)

Probably Han Dynasty (206 B.C.–220 A.D.)

Brownish-olive patina : Height 10″

BRITISH MUSEUM, LONDON

This bronze is decorated with a close pattern of *hui*-motives of a type which is more generally associated with the period of the Warring States (481–206 B.C.); but it was dug up in the Dane John at Canterbury, and while it is sufficiently difficult to account for its presence in England even in the first or second century A.D. as the property of some rich and cultured Roman, it is quite impossible to conceive it being brought here before that. That it was a treasured possession of some mediaeval owner is on the face of it extremely unlikely, and how it found its way here at all is a mystery, but that it did so at some time reasonably close to its manufacture seems probable.

15*a*. CLOAK-HOOK
Han Dynasty (206 B.C.–220 A.D.)

Silver inlaid with turquoise : Length 4"

MR H. OPPENHEIM, LONDON

A stalking leopard.

15*b*. PLAQUE
Han Dynasty (206 B.C.–220 A.D.)

Gilt bronze : Height 3·25"

MR H. OPPENHEIM, LONDON

A bucking ram.

15*c*. ELK
Han Dynasty (206 B.C.–220 A.D.)

Jade : Height 2"

MR H. OPPENHEIM, LONDON

Brownish-yellow jade with a trace of red pigment.

15*d*. CLOAK-HOOK
Han Dynasty (206 B.C.–220 A.D.)

Bronze inlaid with silver and gold : Length 3·25"

MR H. OPPENHEIM, LONDON

Reddish-brown patina; phoenix forms, the eye of the main head inlaid
with a blue glass paste.

16. STONE RELIEF FROM A TOMB
Han Dynasty (206 B.C.–220 A.D.)

Length 42" ; Height 28"

THE LOUVRE, PARIS

This sculpture, a typical example of the Han tomb reliefs of which the
series dated 147–149 A.D. in the Wu Liang cemetery in Shantung, is the
most important, were based on paintings, such as existed in the Ling
Kuang palace, the site of which was about sixteen miles away from the
Wu Liang cemetery. The background is cut away and leaves the figures
standing in relief. Doubt has been thrown on the genuineness of this
slab, but while it is possible that the outlines have been freshened up,
there seems no reason to regard the carving as forged.

17. STONE RELIEF
Han Dynasty (206 B.C.–220 A.D.)

A Phoenix. From the pillars of Ch'en at Chü Hsien in Ss'ŭ-chüan

IN SITU

The phoenix emblem of the South, the Summer and the Morning, is associated with the colour red, the corresponding animals being:

Dragon: East. Spring: Blue.
Tiger: West. Autumn: White.
Tortoise: North. Winter: Black.

References: Ashton, *Introduction*, etc., pl. x, and p. 31. Photo. Mission Ségalen (by permission of the Musée Guimet).

Han Dynasty

18a. SILK WEAVING
Han Dynasty (206 B.C.–220 A.D.)

Dark brown and buff: Height 15″

SCIENTIFIC ACADEMY, LENINGRAD

This interesting textile with its obvious bearing on landscape painting of the period can hardly have been used except for some decorative purpose, such as a curtain pelmet or tent-band. It forms part of the hoard found at Noin-Ola in Mongolia by Kozloff in 1924–25.

Reference: Trever, *Excavations in Northern Mongolia,* pl. 15.

18b. PAIR OF FIGURES
Han Dynasty (206 B.C.–220 A.D.)

Light green jade: Height 2·75″

MRS WALTER SEDGWICK, LONDON

These charming little figures are admirable examples of the effect obtained by the most economical means. Though on so small a scale they are masterpieces of stylized representation.

Han Dynasty

19a. DRINKING-CUP
Han Dynasty, dated 2 B.C.

Painted by Huo for the Shang-lin park

Lacquer: Length 6·8"

SCIENTIFIC ACADEMY, LENINGRAD

The earliest dated example of lacquer known. Similar pieces have been
discovered in Korea.
Kozloff Expedition, 1924–25.

Reference: Trever, *op. cit.,* pl. 30.

19b. SILK-WEAVING
Han Dynasty (206 B.C.–220 A.D.)

Width 18"

SCIENTIFIC ACADEMY, LENINGRAD

Woven in green and buff on a red ground, the pattern of this silk shows
a relation with the designs on inlaid bronze and also on a few pieces of
lacquer.
Kozloff Expedition, 1924–25.

Reference: Yetts, *Burlington Magazine,* April, 1926.

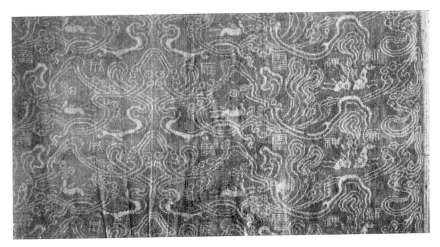

20*a*. HILL-JAR
Han Dynasty (206 B.C.–220 A.D.)

Glazed earthenware : Height 8″

VICTORIA AND ALBERT MUSEUM, LONDON

This type of jar, so called from the representation on the lid of a mountain, is often found in Han tombs. The subject may be connected with the Taoist Isles of the Blest in the Western Ocean. The base in this case has tigers and *tao t'ieh* mask handles in relief, while the whole vessel is covered with a dark green lead glaze which has partially turned silvery through decomposition.

20*b*. FIGURES PLAYING A GAME
Han Dynasty (206 B.C.–220 A.D.)

Group in glazed earthenware : Height about 8″

BRITISH MUSEUM, LONDON

This delightful group is executed in the typical earthenware of the Han period, covered with a green lead glaze, which has turned silvery through decomposition.

21*a*. VASE
Han Dynasty (206 B.C.–220 A.D.)

Painted earthenware: Height 14"

BRITISH MUSEUM, LONDON (EUMORFOPOULOS
COLLECTION)

Grey unglazed earthenware, painted in unfired red, green, and white pigments with bands of cloud ornament, in the central example of which mythical animals are introduced. The design should be compared with that on the textile (*Pl.* 19*b*), showing the close affinity between textile and ceramic design which has always existed in China.

21*b*. FIGURE OF A MAN
3rd–5th century A.D.

Unglazed earthenware: Height 28·5"

BRITISH MUSEUM, LONDON (EUMORFOPOULOS
COLLECTION)

A charming and attractive example of an early tomb figure.

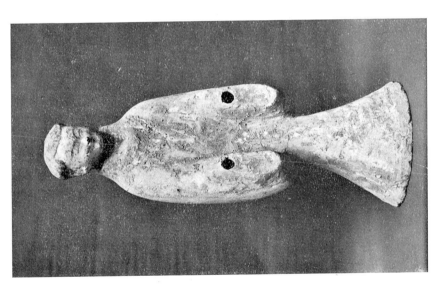

22. TAOIST WORLD OF THE DEAD

2nd century A.D.

Detail from the right-hand triangular clay brick of a pediment in three pieces. Painted al secco *in outline with washes of colour on a white prepared ground. Size: Greatest height 10·5″; greatest width 13″*

BRITISH MUSEUM, LONDON (EUMORFOPOULOS COLLECTION)

These painted bricks come from the entrance to a tomb of the late Han period. The scenes represent the world of the dead as conceived by the Taoists of this period who were firm believers in magic. The drawing is hasty and summary, it being only necessary to represent the scene sufficiently for it to be recognizable. It was afterwards smeared with red paint, which in the realm of magic was considered a lucky colour for the dead. Taoism had sunk low, but there is nevertheless a sureness of vision as well as of touch about these paintings, which prove them to be true work of the imagination. The other-worldliness of the celestial winged stag and the tremendous speed of the cloud chariot harnessed to the stork are successfully represented.

References: L. Binyon, *Catalogue of the George Eumorfopoulos collection of Chinese . . . paintings*, No. 1. O. Fischer, *Die Chinesische Malerei der Han-dynastie*, pp. 77-70; pls. 60-62. *British Museum Quarterly*, vol. x, No. 1.

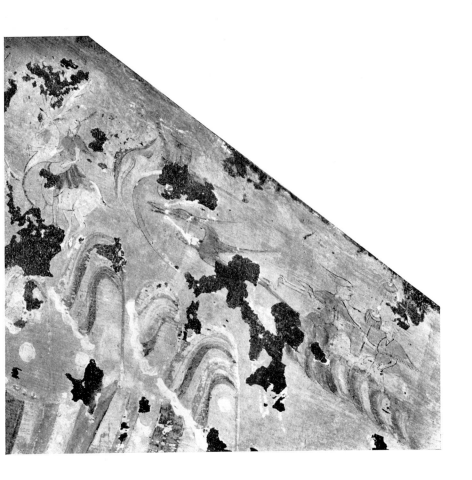

23. PAINTED BRONZE LID
Han Dynasty, 206 B.C.–220 A.D.

Bronze painted in body colour : Diameter 7″

This painted lid is interesting as an example of Han decorative work. The spiralling lines are executed in black, the phoenix in green and blue, the ground being red. The style may be compared with the lacquer finds from Noin-ola (cf. *Pl.* 19*a*) and in more recent times from 'the tomb of the Painted Basket' at Lolang in Korea.

24. ARISTOCRATIC LADIES WATCHING ANIMAL FIGHT IN THE SHANG-LIN PARK
About 3rd century A.D.

Detail from a polychrome painting on hollow bricks excavated from a tomb in the neighbourhood of Lo-yang. The section reproduced is from the reverse of the lintel of the tomb
Size: 19·5 cm. × 29·63 cm. (7·5″ × 11·7″)

MUSEUM OF FINE ARTS, BOSTON

The figures on the lintel are presumably the spectators at the fight represented above between wild animals, apparently a tiger and a boar, such as we know to have taken place at Shanglin, the imperial park in Shensi. On one side are the men, courteous and aloof; on the other side the ladies, elegantly gossiping. The drawing is skilful in a calligraphic way and gives a vivid picture of the elegant and worldly society of the day.

Already can be seen the Chinese genius for spacing.

References: Tomita, *Portfolio*, fols, 1–8. O. Fischer, *Die Chinesische Malerei der Han-dynastie*, pp. 82–83; pl. 71.

PERIOD OF THE WEI TARTARS
(386–557 A.D.)
AND THE SIX DYNASTIES
(220–589 A.D.)

CHRONOLOGY

THE THREE KINGDOMS	220–280 A.D.
THE SIX DYNASTIES	220–589 A.D.
WESTERN AND EASTERN CHIN	265–419 A.D.
THE FIVE DYNASTIES	420–618 A.D.
PERIOD OF THE NORTHERN AND SOUTHERN DYNASTIES:	
Liu Sung ⎫	420–478 A.D.
Southern Ch'i ⎪ *South*	479–501 A.D.
Liang ⎬	502–556 A.D.
Ch'ēn ⎭	557–589 A.D.
Northern Wei ⎫	386–535 A.D.
Eastern Wei ⎪	534–550 A.D.
Western Wei ⎬ *North*	535–557 A.D.
Northern Ch'i ⎪	550–577 A.D.
Northern Chou ⎭	557–581 A.D.
SUI	581–618 A.D.

With the fall of the Han dynasty China was once more split up into a series of states. The history of China has always been a period of prosperity and a period of decadence, followed by a barbarian invasion, which with its influx of fresh blood revivified the failing strength of the nation. Of the various dynasties which came to power during these four centuries the most important were the T'opa Tartars, more usually known as the Wei Tartars, who ruled over the North of China from 386–557 A.D.

BUDDHISM

The most important happening during this period was the establishment in China of Buddhism. While tradition describes its first appearance in China with the Dream of the Emperor Ming Ti, who seeing a golden man fly into the room, was advised that it was the Buddha and was converted in 68 A.D., it is quite uncertain when the first missionaries actually penetrated to China. But in the fourth century, when the Chinese were admitted to the Clergy, the religion really began to be of extreme power. To its success we owe the greater part of the figure-sculpture of China, which was directly inspired by the popularity of the Mahayanist canon of the Buddhist religion, a creed holding out the prospect of re-birth in a paradise presided over by one of the powerful deities such as Avalokitesvara, the God of Mercy, later identified with Kuan-yin, the Chinese Goddess of the same power, or Amitabha, Ruler of the Western Paradise. The sculptors carved in stone, in wood and in lacquer and cast their figures in bronze, gilding it with a pale tone of gold of great beauty. Most of these works are votive and by means of the many dated inscriptions it is possible to follow the development of the style; the aesthetic culmination of the period is about 520 A.D. Of the several important groups of rock-cut images, that of Yün-kang at Ta t'ung-fu in Shansi is the most important (*Pl.* 33). The dates in these caves range from about 460 A.D. to about the middle of the sixth century and the figures show the influence of Indian models, though the actual types are probably Chinese, as the Wei Tartars were devoted admirers of everything Chinese. Much of the carving was probably done by workers from the Buddhist colony of Tun-huang on the western borders of China from which 30,000 families were transported in 439 A.D. to the capital P'in-ch'eng.

CAVE SCULPTURE

The type of figure is marked, with high head and long neck, eyes carved in narrow slits, the body a lay-figure on which is placed a decorative pattern of pleats and folds. The feeling that the god is an awful divinity is very clear and it is hardly before the sixth century that this emotion begins to relax and an air of sympathy to soften the treatment of these galaxies of saints. But the sculptor in his working out of the patterns of the robes displays such a feeling for design and movement that the stiffness of his figures is hardly noticeable. The fluttering draperies, the pleated folds, are often combined with a masterly direction and in some of the smaller bronzes achieve as near decorative perfection as is possible.

ANIMAL STYLE

At the same time the style of animal representation is undergoing a change. The irruption of Central Asian elements with the barbarians transforms the simple and elegant Han formula into a complicated and savage restlessness. In small bronzes compositions of writhing forms, on mirror-backs elaborate zones of swirling animals and human forms (*Pl.* 25a), seem to mark the uncertainties that so often occur in the aesthetic values of any transitional period. But the restless style is uplifted by an exuberant vitality, which often carries these new types of design to a successful conclusion. If, at times, we cannot but regret the task the artist has set himself, we cannot but admire the spirit, which has enabled him to carry it through. Towards the close of the period this tremendous vitality finds outlet in some really splendid examples of monumental animal sculpture, the great lions from the Royal tombs of the Liang dynasty (502–557 A.D.) outside Nanking.[1] Heavy in form, with great tongues lolling out, huge heads, and crouching bodies, the sculptor has yet invested them with a vitality, which effectively lightens the unwieldy mass of the stone.

KU K'AI-CHIH

Though the names of earlier painters are preserved, Ku K'ai-chih (*b*. 344) is the first whom we can envisage as a real person. All the early histories of Chinese painting make long references to him, and he is represented by a painting in the British Museum, probably an original, a long silk roll illustrating the 'Admonitions of the Preceptress'. Ku K'ai-chih lived at a time when Buddhism was making great progress in China and he is known to have painted Buddhist subjects, including a colossal wall-painting of Vimalakirti; but it is difficult to imagine what these can have been like. Many stories are told to illustrate the originality of his views and his exaggerated ways of stating them. How far is the British Museum painting an index to the state of painting in China about 400 A.D.? It is arranged in nine sections, divided by calligraphy, and illustrates the 'Lessons of the Palace Instructress' composed by Chang Hua about a hundred years earlier. It thus follows an archaic form and is an example of a didactic style of painting which is hardly represented in Europe. Examining it more closely we find that the subject is treated with pedantic attention to detail and feeling for the subject. But we can see that there is nothing false or not realized in the relationship of the persons. It succeeds, where the Han brick paintings at Boston fail, in setting down most subtly the psychological attitude of the figures to one another. Like Watteau, Ku K'ai-chih was able to state in his paintings something true for all time under the superficial forms of his day; for he moved in a society that was literary in its tastes and aristocratic in its organization, amusing itself with poetic contests and the making of acrostics. But, far from being decadent, this society was full of vitality and ready, at the favourable moment, to develop the great T'ang civilization. In such a paradoxical age it is natural to find a painter so contradictory in qualities as Ku K'ai-chih. Though, no doubt, the greatest painter of his age, he must differ in quality rather than in kind from his contemporaries whose work has not survived. Indeed, it is possible to see some-

[1] Ashton, *Introduction, etc.*, pl. 45.

thing of the same hint of a bigger reality beneath the smiling ingenuity of the Wei figures.

With the sixth century, Buddhist sculpture enters on a different phase. The remoteness of the deities has passed and it is as beneficent saints that they begin to be conceived. The forms lose their stiffness and human bodies begin to show beneath the elaborate robes.

LUNG-MĒN CAVES

The Lung-mēn caves in Honan are the best known of all the series of this date in China. The votive inscriptions range from 495 A.D. to the middle of the eighth century and here the influence of the Indian types becomes more apparent. The tall figures with swinging draperies caught across waist or knee, floating scarves and long chains of jewellery, show close affinities with the type of figure which reached its climax in India in the frescoes of the Ajanta caves. In many of the smaller figures, too, this tendency to humanize the aspect of the divinities achieves some lovely compositions, such as the celebrated bronze formerly in the Peytel Collection, of the Divine conversation between Sakya-mūni and Prabhutaratna (*Pl.* 34).

SIX DYNASTIES CERAMICS

In ceramics the period of the Six Dynasties was one of great import-ance; for the development from the simple glazes of the Han dynasty to the complicated types of the T'ang dynasty (618–906 A.D.) cannot have taken place without many intervening stages. But we are somewhat lacking in evidence at present as to exactly how these stages took place. The tomb figurines show many types (*Pl.* 30) which by comparison with the cave-sculptures we can definitely place in this period, some of them singularly beautiful with tall slender bodies and simple flowing robes; they are as a rule of a dark grey body and decorated with touches of un-fired pigment. To this period also almost certainly belongs the so-called proto-porcelain with a hard grey stoneware body and an olive felspathic glaze of a thin quality (*Pl.* 28).

25*a*. MIRROR-BACK
2nd–3rd century A.D.

Bronze: Width 5″

M. LAGRELIUS, STOCKHOLM

25*b*. MIRROR-BACK
(Dated 225 A.D.)

Bronze: Diameter 4·6″

NATIONAL MUSEUM, STOCKHOLM

Dated mirrors are rare and as the transition from the Han style to the more restless patterns of the succeeding period is an extremely complicated and difficult question, this piece with its zone of human figures and writhing monsters is an important document, stylistically.

26. BRONZE DRAGON
3rd–4th century A.D.

Blue-green patina : Length 24″

STOCLET COLLECTION, BRUSSELS

An admirable example of the strength of conception of the animal-representation of the post-Han period.

27. HORSE'S HEAD
Perhaps 4th–5th century A.D.

Glaucous green jade : Height 10"

VICTORIA AND ALBERT MUSEUM, LONDON
(EUMORFOPOULOS COLLECTION)

This lovely piece of sculpture, with its strongly stylized details yet naturalistic conception, while it has affinities of line with the horses shown on the Han relief, yet seems to be more connected in feeling with the great animals of the Liang tombs near Nanking and may with all probability be dated between Han and T'ang. Earthenware figures of horses of this date with detachable heads as in this case are well known.

28. VASE
3rd–5th century A.D.

Porcellanous stoneware : Height 11″

VICTORIA AND ALBERT MUSEUM, LONDON

This vessel, of a reddish body with olive-brown glaze, shows an intermediate stage of hardness between earthenware and porcelain: it belongs to a class often referred to as proto-porcelain.

29. BUFFALO

3rd–5th century A.D.

Unglazed earthenware : Height 10″

MUSEUM FÜR VÖLKERKUNDE, BERLIN

A fine and vigorous example of a tomb-figure.

3O. MAN FEEDING A BIRD
3rd–5th century A.D.

Unglazed earthenware : Height 8″

MR H. OPPENHEIM, LONDON

Grey body painted over a white slip with touches of colour.

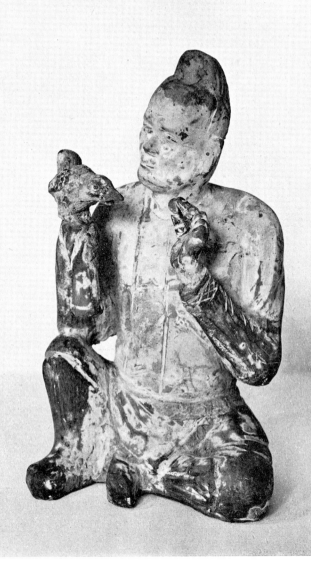

31. DETAIL FROM THE ADMONITIONS OF THE INSTRUCTRESS

Attributed to Ku K'ai-chih, *4th century A.D.*

The Husband reproaching his Wife. Part of the seventh scene in the painting as it exists today. Painted in ink, with touches of red, on silk. In the part reproduced there are patches near both hands, on the chest and by the feet, which are visible in the reproduction. Some of the other lines, both in red and black, have been gone over, but the face and the fainter lines of the costume, below the waist, are apparently from the hand of the original artist.

Size: Same size as original

The question whether this painting is actually as old as the fourth century A.D. will probably never be decided. But a number of distinguished critics such as Tung Ch'i-ch'ang the famous Chinese connoisseur of the sixteenth century and, more recently, Professor Fukui of Japan, have come to the conclusion that it is of this dating. It apparently belonged to the Sung Emperor Hui Tsung to whose own hand is attributed the text of the remaining part of the Admonitions, which follows immediately after the painting itself. This is certainly in the style of Hui Tsung, but Professor Yashiro has recently shown that it is probably by the Tartar Emperor Chang Tsung about seventy years later. In any case such external evidence from inscriptions cannot be conclusive, while seals were commonly forged.

The style of the painting itself remains the final and only primary criterion. The British Museum scroll agrees in style with what we expect of a painting of the fourth century, coming between the Han reliefs and the T'ang pictures. It must be admitted that it does not quite correspond with what we should imagine Ku K'ai-chih's style to have been from the literary sources. He seems to have been poetic and imaginative; stronger in conception than execution. In the Admonitions the characterization and the beauty of line are equally matched.

Reference: Waley, *Introduction to the Study of Chinese Painting*, pp. 54–59.

32. VASE AND COVER

Six Dynasties or early T'ang ; 6th–7th century A.D.

Earthenware : Height 13"

MR H. OPPENHEIM, LONDON

Painted over a white slip with a design of birds and chrysanthemums in black, white and red.

33. BUDDHA MAITREYA
Wei Tartar, probably 5th century

Limestone statue : Height 57·5"

METROPOLITAN MUSEUM, NEW YORK

This statue is from the Yün-kang caves in Shansi. With its stylized pleats, crossed legs and smiling face with high cheek-bones, it is a characteristic example of the early Wei Tartar type.

34. GILT-BRONZE GROUP: PRABHUTARATNA AND SAKYA-MUNI

Wei Tartar Dynasty, dated 518 A.D.

Height: 10·25"

LOUVRE, PARIS

This little group touches perhaps the high-water mark of these small votive pieces. The poses, the arrangement of the draperies, the use of the narrow tapering mandorlas, the proportions of the stand are all admirable; the modelling of the heads, the long tapering hands and feet, further accentuate the flickering design of flames engraved on the borders of the mandorlas.

.

35. VOTIVE STELE
Western Wei : dated 554 A.D.

Stone : Height 84″

MUSEUM OF FINE ARTS, BOSTON

In the top scene is the conversation between Prabhutaratna and Sakya-muni, with the Buddha in meditation on one side and in retreat in a cave in the other. Below is Sakya-muni with Ananda and Kaçyapa with attendant Bodhisattvas, and below that carvings of the principal Donors.

36. MARBLE TORSO: SAKYA-MUNI
Probably 6th–7th century

Height: 4' 9"

VICTORIA AND ALBERT MUSEUM, LONDON

This torso is under strong Indian influence. It is possible that it represents the type of the celebrated sandalwood image made by King Udayana of the Buddha in his lifetime, a copy of which was brought back by Hsüan Tsang in 654 A.D., another copy of which reached the Emperor Wu Ti of the Liang dynasty in 511 A.D., and the type of which is also thought to be represented by the celebrated image in the Seiroji Temple, Japan.

T'ANG DYNASTY

(618–906 A.D.)

The short-lived Sui dynasty (581–618 A.D.) was not only important for its political significance in once more uniting the divided kingdoms into one Empire, but also because in a period marked by great luxury—the Emperor Yang Ti rivalled the ninth century Caliph Khumārawayh in Cairo in the splendour of his court—Buddhist sculpture passed through a short phase of extreme elegance, which has often provoked a comparison with the beauties of full European Gothic. A notable example of this date is the bronze altar-piece from the Tuan Fang collection, now in the Museum of Fine Arts, Boston, and dated 593 A.D.[1]

With the T'ang dynasty (618–906 A.D.) China entered on its greatest period of political prosperity. Under the founder of the dynasty T'ai Tsung (627–649 A.D.) and later under Ming Huang (713–755 A.D.) the borders of the Empire were extended to India and the Caspian. With the close connection with India and the pilgrimages of such celebrated monks as Hsüan Tsang, who returned in 645 A.D. with a group of copies of famous Indian images, Buddhism attained its greatest period of power, in spite of the adoption of Taoism as the official religion.

T'ANG SCULPTURE

Buddhist sculpture has now reached its zenith. The iconography and gestures have become settled and individual conceptions begin to appear (Pl. 37). The fall of the drapery is determined by the position, while the body itself begins to be carved with an attempt at naturalistic modelling (Pl. 39). The conventional poses begin to alter and movement is sometimes allowed; the stiff frontal aspect of the previous centuries is no longer adhered to. The most beautiful of these statues were to be found in the T'ien-lung shan series of sculptures in Shansi, many of which have now been removed to Western collections. A tremendous religious persecution in 845 A.D. destroyed an enormous quantity of images and a different religious and philosophical outlook on life diminished their popularity in the succeeding dynasty.

Animal sculpture was produced in large quantities under the T'ang dynasty. It is highly realistic with an emphasis on the outstanding quality of the animal concerned. Thus the wild animals tearing their prey will be carved with a savage ferocity of expression (Pl. 41b), with an accentuation of the muscles under the skin, while the domestic ox will show the placidity and soft contours characteristic of the tame household beast. At the same time many of the monumental pieces are splendid examples of sculpture on a large scale. The celebrated slabs from the

[1] Ashton, *Introduction to Chinese Sculpture*, pl. xlii.

tomb of T'ai Tsung in the University Museum,[1] Philadelphia, represent the Emperor's favourite chargers and are executed from the drawings of Yen Li-pēn, the well-known painter. Carved in relief, in a frame-work cut back in the stone, the compositions fill the rectangular space in an extremely satisfactory way, while the technical accomplishment is of a high order.

The tomb figurines of horses, camels, musicians, etc., in which a certain sculptural element is clear, are on rather a different plane. Though they are often extremely well modelled, the interest which attached to them when they first appeared in Europe has worn off and it must be admitted that like the Greek terracottas from Tanagra they show competence and often charm, but reflect too much the great material prosperity of the T'ang period; they may be regarded as commercial products rather than as works of art.

T'ANG CERAMICS

From a ceramic point of view the period is one of great importance. At the beginning of the dynasty we see the development of the Six Dynasties type of figurine with dark grey body and slight colouring in unfired pigment into a large and varied group (*Pl.* 55) with a refined buff-coloured body decorated for the most part with coloured lead glazes of considerable beauty, the colouring of grass-green, orange-yellow or deep blue being achieved by staining with metallic oxides.

These methods of colouring were also employed on the vessels, for which a much more varied repertory of decoration was used. These vessels, whether covered urns for grain, ewers of various shapes, tripods or bowls, are notable for the strength of form and grace of proportion. The consistency of the body varies from a soft earthenware to a much harder type, which may more fittingly be called stoneware and in some cases approaches very close to porcelain. The lead glazes with their rich staining were fully controlled by the potters, who were able to achieve astonishingly complicated patterns, sometimes by mere staining, sometimes by a formal design engraved in the paste which encloses the different tinctures in the manner of a cloisonné enamel (*Pl.* 53). Apart from these colour effects, the patterns of the T'ang potters were mainly achieved by engraving under the glaze freely drawn floral and palmette designs (*Pl.* 57), by simple stamped or applied motives, and occasionally by more elaborate moulded or stamped designs of marked Hellenistic or Iranian influence. Towards the close of the dynasty a high-fired porcelain with buff, white (*Pl.* 56) or celadon glaze was produced, which is very difficult to distinguish from that of the succeeding period, but fragments

[1] Ashton, *op. cit.*, pl. xlvii.

recovered from the site of the city of Sāmārrā on the Tigris, deserted in 883 A.D., make it perfectly clear that this type of ware was being produced as early as the ninth century.

METAL-WORK

In metal-work the T'ang smiths were not behind their predecessors, though the form of decoration of ritual bronzes ceases to have any interest compared with the earlier specimens. But both in mirrors and in jewellery their skill is extreme. In mirror-backs a sculptural quality (*Pl. 52b*) succeeds the restless energy of the Six Dynasties patterns and in particular in the well-known 'grape-vine' design the control of outline and the technical skill of the deep cutting is first-rate. In others with hunting and animal motives the sense of movement, as well as the composition of these motives, seems to reflect Sasānian design (*Pl. 52a*). This again is noticeable in some of the smaller silver and gold objects, which in their freely-drawn scroll-work carry all the liveliness of the Sasānian silver (*Pl. 47a*). Some of the cosmetic boxes and cups (*Pl. 46b*) with elaborate patterns against a dotted ground are particularly beautiful.

TEXTILES

This Sasānian influence may also be traced in the few textiles we have left dating from this period. Here the use of roundels (*Pl. 42*), confronted animals and intervening palmette forms comes straight from Persia, absorbing elements of Turkestan—a connection easily traceable in the frescoes from Kyzīl now in the Museum für Völkerkunde in Berlin —and sinicizing these elements in a very marked way in such pieces as the banner of Prince Shotoku in the Tokio Museum with its Bahram Gūr motive transplanted into Chinese soil. But indeed it is hardly surprising that this strong Sasānian element should be present, as, apart from the commercial relations between the two countries, the last Sasānian Emperor fled to Lo-yang, where he lived till his death.

LACQUER

In the Imperial Shōsō-in or Treasure house at Nāra in Japan is preserved a large collection of objects, the main bulk of which was deposited by the widow of the Emperor Shomu in 756 A.D. Chinese taste seems to have had a considerable vogue in Japanese Court circles at that period and many of these pieces, if not exported from China, must have been made by Chinese workmen on the spot. These decorative pieces are among the most remarkable things we have left from this date. A series of wooden musical instruments (*Pl. 45*) and gaming-boards (*Pl. 44*), inlaid with mother of pearl and coloured, are fine examples of design, as are some panels of bark-cloth with resist-printed patterns of confronted animals and floral forms executed in colours of the most harmonious combinations (*Pl.* 43*a*). A number of lacquer objects (*Pl.* 47*b*) also exist, some of them of considerable importance.

Lacquer is one of the oldest arts in China. The essential element in lacquer is the natural gum of *rhus vernicifera*, which is coloured to the various tints required for use. This material is then painted in successive coats over a foundation of wood, metal or papier-mâché and is ready for decoration with painting (*hua ch'i*) or by carving (*tiao ch'i*). In addition, a certain amount of relief work over gesso was sometimes employed (*ch'iang chin*) while inlay of mother of pearl (*lo tien*) was common. One of the most important centres of the industry in ancient times was Chia-hsing fu, in the province of Chēkiang; later Soochow and Peking were the chief centres.

PAINTING

Just as in other departments of life, so in painting, it is to the T'ang age that the Chinese have always looked back as their period of classic achievement. It is therefore extremely tantalizing to have so little by which we can form an opinion of the justness of this reputation. Now that many pictures that have been for centuries attributed, especially in Japan, to the T'ang period, and a far larger number of less august pedigree have been brought down by scholars to a more recent date, the numbers of generally accepted T'ang paintings is extremely small. Two or three silk rolls only, some Buddhist paintings preserved in Japan, other Buddhist frescoes and paintings on silk found at Tun-huang in Chinese Turkestan and other sites in Central Asia, and some objects decorated with landscapes in the Shōsō-in in Japan—these are almost all that we can point to as primary evidence for the T'ang style.

Of the silk rolls the most important is a picture of 'Thirteen Emperors' from the Han to the Sui period, now preserved in the Boston Museum of Fine Arts. The figures in it are arranged in distinct groups, each of which is dominated by an Emperor who is represented on a larger scale than the attendants about him. Owing to this device, which is reminiscent of the Han reliefs and may be a primitive survival, the picture gives an impression of majesty and weight which is enhanced by the introduction of forceful modelling for the principal figures. According to an early inscription attached to the painting, one, at least, of these groups is by Yen Li-pēn while the others are later copies; but it is now thought that about half the roll may be by his hand. Yen Li-pēn (*d.* 673) is recorded in the literary sources as one of the greatest of the early T'ang painters. As has been mentioned, he designed the sculptures of horses in high relief for the tomb of the Emperor T'ai Tsung (627–49). Their outstanding quality is realism, and in execution the scroll of the Emperor is realistic, though this is partly concealed by the hieratic arrangement, which is no doubt traditional. It is not therefore wholly representative of early T'ang painting. In another painting, 'Listening to Music', attributed to Chou Fang, of which one version is reproduced by Mr. Waley, the attempt at rendering people in space is more successful. The interest in the realistic representation of objects as filling a certain amount of space seems to be the first quality of T'ang painting. Its achievement, we may suppose, was rather on the formal side of composition than in subtlety of line or of characterization.

Its accomplishment in this way may be seen best, perhaps, in another roll at Boston, which, though not an original of the T'ang period, must be by a very good copyist of the eleventh century and reproduce a lost original by Yen Li-pēn. It represents the 'Collating of Classic Texts' (Pl. 59), and the relation of the figures to the ground and to one another in it is extremely satisfying.

WU TAO-TZŬ

But it is when we turn to the Buddhist paintings that we feel we should be approaching the central theme of T'ang art. Partly because of its foreign origin, partly because of its hieratic requirements, but most of all probably because of its popular contacts, Buddhist painting in China has followed a course rather apart from the rest. Its most flourishing period was in the first two hundred years of the T'ang dynasty, and the greatest artist of this age was first and foremost a Buddhist painter. Wu Tao-tzŭ (about 680–about 740) is said to have painted more than three hundred Buddhist frescoes in the palaces of Ch'ang-an and Lo-yang. These perished, with much of the rest of the great T'ang Buddhist art, during the persecution of 841 to 845. Nothing now remains of his work. He is said to have used a violent, sweeping style, his draperies blown out, as if caught in the wind. Since there is no trace of such a violent style in later Buddhist painting, nor in the five paintings of patriarchs by an artist named Li Chēn, carried back to Japan by Kobo Daishi in 807 and now preserved at Kyoto, Professor Pelliot has argued convincingly that these references are only to be taken in a relative way. We must therefore suppose that while keeping a free brushstroke Wu sought for plastic effect. The best preserved of Li Chēn's paintings would be an example of this style. It is a superb combination of realism with hieratic remoteness, of bold conception with delicate execution.

T'ang Dynasty

TUN-HUANG

The paintings at Tun-huang cover a period of about five hundred years, from the sixth century to the beginning of the eleventh. Within these years the dating of the wall-paintings is a matter of conjecture and some disagreement: but a number of the paintings on silk and paper recovered by Sir Aurel Stein and M. Pelliot, and now in the British Museum, in Paris or in Delhi, are dated and it is possible to place them all between the years 729 and 1030. The wall-paintings show the development of the Buddhist style from a simple flat arrangement in narrative bands (Cave 135: sixth century), through a period of majesty where the figures have weight and scale, but stand in a purely hieratic relation to one another (Caves 77, 146 and 70: Early T'ang), to the later T'ang period, from the eighth century onwards, where the interest is in the very complex composition (e.g. Caves 31, 139a). The artist is now concerned to give an architectural unity to the scenes by arranging the figures on terraces in a way that calls out all his ingenuity in perspective. To give greater reality to his figures he paints them with draperies swaying as if in movement, even though this is not really possible in the composition that he has created. But their greatest quality is, no doubt, as superb wall-covering. Not only is the colouring rich but the treatment of the wall-space is highly satisfactory. There is no attempt at that illusionism which would make the wall disappear as in Roman wall-painting nor at its exploitation as a means of diversifying a flat surface with architectural features which might serve as niches for figures, as in High Renaissance and Baroque painting. As Dr. Bachhofer has pointed out, the wall is given a unity by the constant change of the viewpoint of the spectator, so that wherever he looks he seems to be opposite to that particular part of the picture. The paintings on silk all belong to this third period and the larger ones do not differ at all from the wall-paintings (Pl. 49). The smaller banners no doubt reproduce the Buddhist masterpieces painted in China a few years earlier. For there is no reason to believe in the isolation of Tun-huang or that the paintings executed there, which do not show the strong influence from India to which the centre was naturally exposed, differ at all in style or very greatly in quality from the contemporary art of China. This is the same style in which the great frescoes of Wu Tao-tzŭ were painted.

WANG WEI

The greatest landscape painter under the T'ang dynasty was Wang Wei (b. 699; d. 759). Since no painting with any title to be by him survives, and, since as early as the eleventh century it was already almost impossible to find one, it is not easy to say what his style was really like. But we know something about his career as a courtier and about his reputation. He is the first of the long series of painters who were also poets. In his poetry he followed classic lines and was not so free or vigorous as his great contemporaries Li Po or Tu Fu. But in painting he is said to have been an innovator and was later regarded as the founder of the Southern School, the significance of which will be discussed in the next section. The origin of landscape painting was in map making, and in Wang Wei's time the traditional form was the decorative and minute style known as 'blue, green and gold' painting. Many later pictures exist to show us what this dry style of painting was like. Wang Wei discarded such bright colours and painted in washes usually over an outline drawing instead. But at the beginning of his life he seems to have painted in the old style. In the British Museum is a long roll representing Wang Wei's estate on the river Wang; it is said to be a copy by the fourteenth century artist Chao Mēng-fu after Wang Wei. Though this copy is rather lifeless it is possible to imagine a more sensitive original behind it, and it is painted in washes of blue and green.

The composition is built up, hill behind hill, in a way that gives an impression of grandeur and sublimity. Perhaps nearer in style of execution to Wang Wei, as they are much nearer in date, are the landscapes introduced into the background of the Tun-huang paintings (*Pl. 50*). These naturally lack the individual touch of a great painter, but sometimes, as in the detail reproduced, they attain a real grandeur. The outstanding character of this style seems to be an attempt to render distance naturally and to give form to hills and trees. It is descriptive rather than romantic and, like an epic, relies on a cumulative effect of many details rather than on any more dramatic stroke.

37. SAKYA-MUNI AS AN ASCETIC
T'ang Dynasty? (618–906 A.D.)

Dry Lacquer figure: Height 18"

INSTITUTE OF FINE ARTS, DETROIT

Though the chances of a lacquer figure of this date having survived in such good condition are rather small, and it is perfectly easy to place this figure with its rapt devotional aspect at a later period, it is possible taking into consideration the extraordinary strength of the composition that this may be one of the few surviving pieces of the T'ang period, though it must be admitted that the cutting of the eyes is more nearly related to Sung and Yüan wooden sculpture.

38. KNEELING BODHISATTVA

T'ang Dynasty (probably 8th–9th century)

Limestone statue : Height 22·5"

MR GRENVILLE WINTHROP, NEW YORK

This lovely little figure, strongly influenced by Indian types, certainly belongs to a period after the return of Hsüan Tsang in 645 A.D. with his group of Indian images. It may well be that this statue reflects one of the illustrations of the *Hsi Kuo chih* 'Memorial upon the Western Lands', a work by the sculptor Sung Fa-chih, no copy of which survives, which contained fourteen chapters of illustrations of Indian sculpture.

39. STANDING AMIDA
T'ang Dynasty (probably 8th–9th century)

Marble statue : Height 3′ 2″

PETERS COLLECTION, NEW YORK

This statue belongs to a period of Buddhist sculpture when the relation of the body to the drapery had achieved a naturalistic elegance far removed from the stylized types of the earlier periods. It is probably to be dated not long before the great iconoclastic persecution of 845 A.D.

40. BODHISATTVA

T'ang Dynasty, 8th–9th century

Limestone : Height 5′ 10·5″

MR AND MRS J. D. ROCKEFELLER, JR., NEW YORK

This lovely torso, perhaps the finest example of Buddhist sculpture in existence, owes much to Indian influence—its affinities with the celebrated Sanchi torso in the Victoria and Albert Museum are plain—but the freedom of treatment and the control of modelling and drapery are unusual in Chinese art. Indeed, only in the T'ien-lung shan caves are there any other pieces at all comparable with it. The statue must belong to a period when such individuality was possible, and it is probably not long before the great persecution of 845 A.D. that it must be dated.

41a. STONE LION
T'ang Dynasty (618–906 A.D.)

Height 11"

THE LOUVRE, PARIS

41b. STONE LION DEVOURING ITS PREY
T'ang Dynasty (618–906 A.D.)

Height 10"

THE LOUVRE, PARIS

Admirable examples of the power of the T'ang animal sculptors at expressing the ferocity of wild animals.

42. PANEL FROM A SILK WEAVING FORMING THE COVER OF AN ELBOW-REST
T'ang Dynasty, 8th century

IMPERIAL SHŌSŌ-IN, NĀRA, JAPAN

Simple twill weave, the design in red, yellow and white on a brown ground.

An adaptation of Sasānian textile form to Far Eastern taste; though it is possible that this silk may be Japanese, and not Chinese, the preponderance of Chinese objects among the treasure deposited in 756 A.D. seems to point to a Chinese origin.

43*a*. PANEL

T'ang Dynasty (8th century)

Bark-cloth stencilled in olive-green, dull red and brown on a buff ground

IMPERIAL SHŌSŌ-IN, NĀRA, JAPAN

A fabric primarily used for lining of chests, etc. The design, strongly influenced by the well-known Middle-Eastern motive of confronted animals on either side of the sacred hōm-tree, shows the individual adaptation characteristic of all good designing based on a borrowed source.

43*b*. DESIGN FOR AN EMBROIDERY ON SILK, PARTIALLY EXECUTED IN KINGFISHER FEATHERS

T'ang Dynasty (8th century)

Height 53·5″

IMPERIAL SHŌSŌ-IN, NĀRA, JAPAN

44. TWO PANELS FROM A GAMING-BOARD
T'ang Dynasty, 8th century

Lacquered wood inlaid with mother of pearl

Length of each panel (about) 4·8"

IMPERIAL SHŌSŌ-IN, NĀRA, JAPAN

The extraordinary vitality and humour of these little inlays mark them out even at a period when most applied art was on an extremely high level.

45*a*. MIRROR
T'ang Dynasty (8th century)

Bronze, encrusted with mother of pearl, painted red and black

Diameter 12·85″

IMPERIAL SHŌSŌ-IN, NĀRA, JAPAN

45*b*. BACK OF A MUSICAL INSTRUMENT
T'ang Dynasty (8th century)

Diameter 15·35″

Cherry-wood inlaid with mother of pearl, painted in red and green

IMPERIAL SHŌSŌ-IN, NĀRA, JAPAN

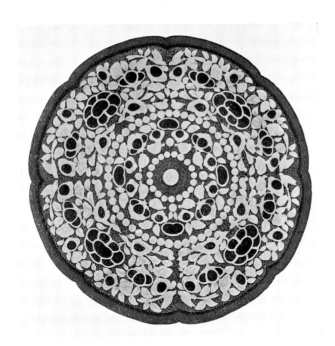

46a. KETTLE
Probably 6th century

Silver : Height of bowl, 3·4"

MRS WALTER SEDGWICK, LONDON

While related in type of treatment to the large group of slightly later silver-work of the T'ang dynasty (618–906 A.D.) the type of figure on this kettle is clearly connected both by style of costume and expression of face with the period of the great stone steles of the sixth century, on which the figures of donors provide a close analogy.

46b. WINE CUP
T'ang Dynasty (618–906 A.D.)

Silver : Height 4·3" Diameter 3·4"

MRS WALTER SEDGWICK, LONDON

Engraved with a hunting scene. The delicately engraved metal-work of the T'ang dynasty is distinguished by its freely drawn patterns executed as a rule against a dotted ground. In this group this cup is an outstanding example both for the quality of its execution and the vitality of its design.

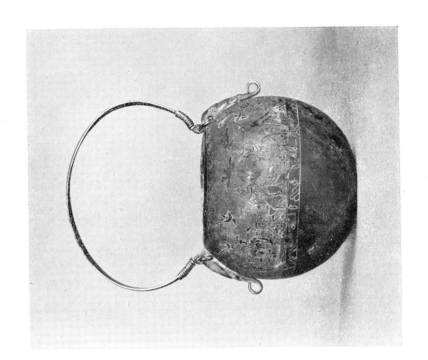

47a. GOLD DISH
T'ang Dynasty (618–906 A.D.)

Diameter 3·8"

MR F. GUTMANN, HEEMSTEDE, HOLLAND

47b. WOODEN CHEST
T'ang Dynasty, 8th century

Height about 12"

IMPERIAL SHŌSŌ-IN, NĀRA, JAPAN

Painted in gold lacquer pigment with a phoenix design.

48. EMBROIDERED BANNER
T'ang Dynasty : 8th–9th century

Silk on linen, chain and split stitch : Height 8'

BRITISH MUSEUM, LONDON

The banner in red, yellow and black represents Sakya-muni attended by Ananda and Kaçyapa and two Bodhisattvas; below are donors. Part of the hoard found by Sir Aurel Stein in the Caves of the Thousand Buddhas at Tun-huang.

References: Stein, *Serindia*, pp. 878 *et. seq.*, 983 *et. seq.: The Thousand Buddhas*, pp. 48 *et. seq.* Waley, *Catalogue of Printings recovered from Tun-huang*, p. 209.

49. MANDALA OF THE THOUSAND-ARMED AVALOKITESVARA
9th century A.D.

Recovered by Sir Aurel Stein from the Caves of the Thousand Buddhas, Tun-huang, Chinese Turkestan. Full colour, on silk

(Upper portion) Size: 60" × 70"

BRITISH MUSEUM (STEIN COLLECTION, NO. 32)

In the centre at the top is Bhaishajya: on either side two Bodhisattvas are seated. They are distinctly Indian in type, with narrow waists and bodies slightly bent. Below is a host of lesser Bodhisattavas and musicians of entirely Chinese type. Rising above them are the figures of Samantabhadra on his vehicle the elephant, and Manjusri on his lion. Each is attended by a very dark figure, evidently intended for an Indian though not of Indian type.

Such large silk banner paintings as this, which must originally have measured about 12 feet by 6 feet, are almost identical in style and colouring, as well as in subject, with the contemporary wall paintings, reproduced by Professor Pelliot.

These are the palaces of the blest where music is always played, as the sacred lotus blossom falls through the air. As has been pointed out above, the T'ang artists who treated these Buddhist subjects had so good a sense of composition on a large scale that they were able to arrange this multitude of figures in an orderly and impressive way. The system is eminently hieratic, but a spatial range is provided by the architectural framework. This and the landscape are purely Chinese and owe nothing to Indian influence. At the top in the corners can be seen mountains rising peak behind peak.

References: Serindia, pl. lix. Thousand Buddhas, pl. iii.

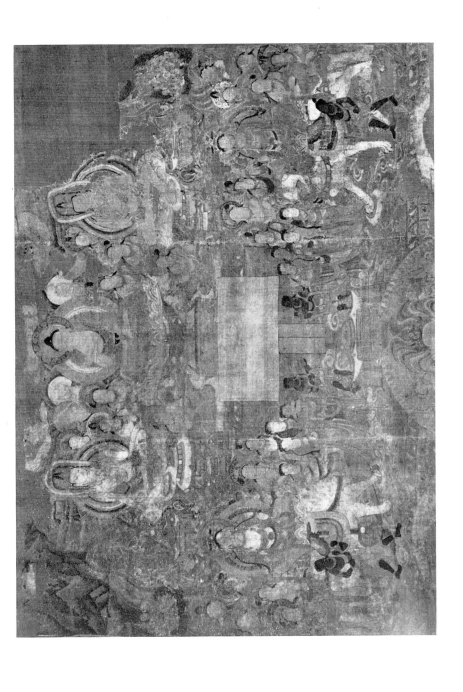

T'ang Dynasty

5O. LANDSCAPE
9th century A.D.

Detail from the last plate
Size: 22" × 11"

BRITISH MUSEUM (STEIN COLLECTION, NO. 32)

Though landscape only plays a subordinate part in the Buddhist paintings from Tun-huang, the formal mountains, introduced into many of the
border pictures illustrating scenes from the life of the Buddha arranged
round the large banners, or in series one below the other on the small
banners, must reflect the authentic landscape style of the great T'ang
painters. The present example is more finished than usual and is almost
strong enough to stand alone. The system of washes corresponds with
what we know from the literary sources of the style of Wang Wei.

51. AVALOKITESVARA AS THE GUIDE OF SOULS
10th century A.D.

Recovered by Sir Aurel Stein from the caves of the Thousand Buddhas, Tun-huang, Chinese Turkestan. Full colours on silk

Size : 31·5" × 21"

BRITISH MUSEUM (STEIN COLLECTION, NO. 47)

Among the paintings of the Stein Collection this stands out as an accomplished and striking design. It is generally accepted as being a direct copy from an original of the seventh or eighth century and may be as near as we can get to the style of Wu Tao-tzü. The lady following the Bodhisattva is dressed in the costume of the early eighth century as we know it from the embroidered picture in the Shōsō-in (*Pl. 43b*) and from a fragment found by Sir Aurel Stein in the Astana cemetery in Turfan in 1923. Compare also the figures of the *Ladies preparing newly-woven silk* below (*Pl. 60*). How little there is of anything but Chinese in this painting it is easy to see if we compare it with a similar painting of far more Indian treatment in the Musée Guimet (Grousset, *China*, fig. 211). The figure of this Bodhisattva, solid yet borne on a cloud, is realistically treated yet appears remote and majestic. Behind is one of the palaces of the blest. The inscription reads: 'Bodhisattva who leads the way'. This designation is usually referred to Khsitigarbha (Jizo) and is actually taken for him by Seiichi Taki in spite of the fact that he wears the full jewellery of a Bodhisattva instead of being represented as a monk with a shaven crown as he should be as Jizo. Mr Waley, however, is unwilling to accept this identification and considers the phrase equally applicable to Avalokitesvara.

References: Serindia, pl. lxxi. *Kokka*, No. 383.

引路菩

T'ang Dynasty

52a. MIRROR-BACK
T'ang Dynasty (618–906 A.D.)

Blackish bronze with green patination : Diameter 6″

THE LOUVRE, PARIS

The design of horsemen hunting a boar and a lion probably derives from the well-known Bahram Gūr motive of Sasānian silver.

52b. MIRROR
T'ang Dynasty (619–906 A.D.)

Silvered-bronze with green patination : Diameter 8·25″

MR RAYMOND A. BIDWELL, SPRINGFIELD,
MASSACHUSETTS, U.S.A.

An extraordinarily brilliant example of strong design and fine *repoussé* work.

T'ang Dynasty

53. DISH
T'ang Dynasty (618–906 A.D.)

Glazed earthenware : Diameter 13″

VICTORIA AND ALBERT MUSEUM, LONDON
(EUMORFOPOULOS COLLECTION)

Buff body, the field covered with a clear glaze stained green and orange, the medallion and cloud forms outlined by engraving which keeps the colours from mixing. The technique of these washes is akin to that of *cloisonné* enamel, which, however, was not known in China at so early a date.

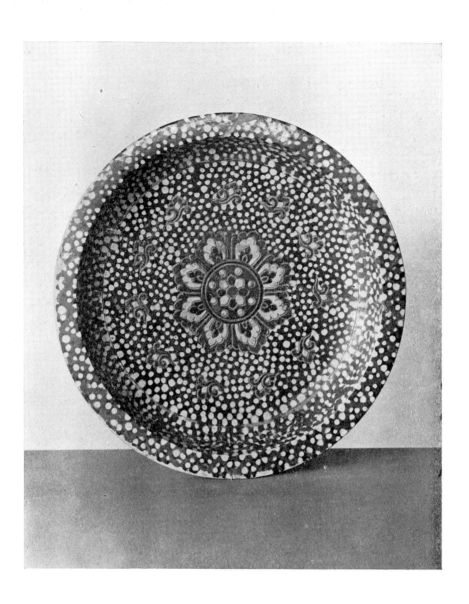

54. DISH
T'ang Dynasty (618–906 A.D.)

Glazed earthenware : Diameter 10″

VICTORIA AND ALBERT MUSEUM, LONDON

Painted in green and yellow glaze washes on a white ground with a lotus and butterflies. This charming dish, unlike most T'ang polychrome pieces, does not achieve its design by a controlled staining of a transparent glaze, but shows clearly the use of some such instrument as a brush.

55. FIGURE OF A LADY
T'ang Dynasty (618–906 A.D.)

Glazed earthenware : Height 12"

VICTORIA AND ALBERT MUSEUM, LONDON
(EUMORFOPOULOS COLLECTION)

Reddish body covered with a transparent glaze stained green and orange.
From the illustrations to the eighth century Japanese scrolls, known as
the *Inga Kyō*, it seems plain that this type of T'ang robe was made of
bands of different coloured material sewn together.

56. VASE
T'ang Dynasty (618–906 A.D.)

Porcellanous stoneware : Height 7"

RUTHERSTON COLLECTION, ENGLAND

Buff body, covered with a lightly crackled buff glaze. This piece illustrates admirably the beauty of ceramic form achieved by the T'ang potters in so many of their less elaborate wares.

T'ang Dynasty

57. EWER
Late T'ang Dynasty (9th–10th century)

Porcelain: Height 15·5"

BRITISH MUSEUM, LONDON (EUMORFOPOULOS COLLECTION)

Engraved in the paste with floral designs and covered with a light olive-grey glaze.

Reference: A. D. Brankston : *British Museum Quarterly*, vol. xiii (1939), pp. 46–7.

T'ang Dynasty

58. FRAGMENT OF LINEN
T'ang Dynasty, probably 9th century

*Embroidered in black, yellow, green and blue silk and gold thread;
mainly chain stitch
Height 8"*

MUSEUM FÜR VÖLKERKUNDE, BERLIN

This interesting fragment of embroidery is part of the material found
by Le Coq at Chotschō in Turfan; though it probably represents a type
of work not purely Chinese, to all intents and purposes it can be
reckoned as such.

59. SCHOLARS OF NORTHERN CH'I DYNASTY COLLATING CLASSIC TEXTS

11th century adaptation of a painting by
YEN LI-PĒN (*b. 600; d. 673*)

Scroll painting in ink and light colours on silk
Size : 27·6 cm. × 1·14 m. (10·9″ × 45″)
Detail : 27·6 cm. × 33·0 cm. (10·9″ × 13″)

MUSEUM OF FINE ARTS, BOSTON

In A.D. 556 the Emperor Wên-hsüan of the Northern Ch'i dynasty commanded Fan Sun to collate the Chinese texts for the use of the heir apparent. The Emperor (*d.* 559) was a Tartar, cruel and profligate. His care for letters is therefore all the more significant, and the incident became famous.

The attribution to Yen Li-pēn goes back to a twelfth century note written on the painting itself. But till the late eighteenth century it does not seem to have been regarded as an original by him. It seems best to consider it, with Mr Tomita, a tenth or eleventh century copy after a T'ang original by some good hand in the Northern Sung dynasty.

Yen Li-pēn, the son of a well-known painter, worked with his brother, Yen Li-tē, at the courts of the great Emperors T'ai Tsung (627–49) and Kao Tsung (650–83). He became a high officer of state and a very successful painter and was made Prime Minister in 668. The best known painting attributed to him that survives is the *Thirteen Emperors*, also in the Boston Museum. It is rather a severe and unattractive painting, though there is undeniable power in the line and weight in the handling. The present example is much lighter and must owe a good deal of its charm to its Sung copyist. But it is possible to imagine the statuesque T'ang picture behind it.

References : Boston Bulletin : xxix, pp. 58–63, Aug. 1931. Tomita, *Portfolio*, pls. 46–51. Siren, *History of Early Chinese Painting*, pp. 60–62.

60. LADIES PREPARING NEWLY-WOVEN SILK

After CHANG HSÜAN (*c. 713–42*)

Scroll painting in full colour, on silk; left-hand portion
Size: 37 cm. × 1·453 m. (14·62" × 57·375")
Detail: 37 cm. × 54 cm. (14·62" × 21·125")

MUSEUM OF FINE ARTS, BOSTON

According to an early thirteenth century attribution, a copy by the Emperor Hui Tsung (1082–1135) after the original painting by Chang Hsüan which was then in his possession and is mentioned in the catalogue of his collection. In any case, there must certainly be a T'ang original behind this painting. Such genre subjects taken from everyday life are rather rare in early Chinese painting. But as much of the beauty of this picture seems to be inherent in the occupation as in the placing and realization of the figures. It is one of the most perfect compositions to be found in Chinese painting.

References: Kojiro Tomita, *Museum of Fine Arts, Boston; Portfolio of Chinese Paintings in the Museum (Han to Sung Periods)* 1933, pp. 46, 52–54. O. Siren, *Chinese Paintings in American Collections*, 1927, pls. 5–8. Yukio Yashiro, *Bijutsu Kenkyu*, No. xli, May 1935.

DATES

THE FIVE DYNASTIES	907–960 A.D.
LIAO AND WESTERN LIAO	907–1201 A.D.
NÜ CHIN	1115–1234 A.D.
SUNG	960–1279 A.D.
Northern Sung	960–1127 A.D.
Southern Sung	1127–1279 A.D.

SUNG DYNASTY

(960–1279 A.D.)

It might have been expected that a long and commercially prosperous epoch like the T'ang dynasty would be succeeded by a period of unrest, but this was not so. Though harassed by barbarian invasions the Sung dynasty (960–1279 A.D.), which after a brief interval established its power, maintained its sway for three centuries with a capital first at K'ai-fēng fu in Honan and later in the South at Hang-chow in Chekiang. The Sung dynasty produced the most intellectual civilization the world has ever known. After so much that was material the logical development of thought and method of life must have been in the direction of something more spiritual. In the first place Buddhism underwent a certain change. The most popular form was the Zen creed, a meditative philosophy of Pantheism, practised by an intellectual game of question and answer. The beauty of the pine-tree laden with snow, the wind in the grass, the flight of a bird across the moon, and the leisure to watch them and to meditate on them were the things that attracted the Chinese.

SUNG SCULPTURE

Sculpture naturally fell into disfavour; material images were not to be compared with the mystic qualities of painting. It is true that a group of wooden statues exists of great beauty with graceful outlines and elaborate flowing draperies (*Pl.* 92) and that in local communities image-making still continued, but the chief importance of Sung art lies in its paintings and in its ceramics, where the use of subtle forms and sensuous glazes carried out the ideals of the age.

It is often forgotten that a space of nearly fifty years intervened between the T'ang and Sung dynasties. In this period may have taken place the revolution in the history of ceramics, which had certainly taken effect by the Sung dynasty. We know of two celebrated wares which were invented at this time.

YÜEH WARE[1]

The first the so-called *pi sē* or secret colour ware of the Princes of Yüeh has been recently identified with a type of celadon of which large quantities of fragments have been recovered at Fostât, the site of the old city of Cairo. It is a well-potted type with a grey body and an olive glaze (*Pl.* 73*b*). Decoration consists of designs finely engraved or

[1] See R. L. Hobson in Transactions of the Oriental Ceramic Society, vol. 14 ; and A. D. Brankston in *Burlington Magazine*, Dec. 1938.

carved in the paste and beneath the foot are found small piles of sand adhering. The other ware is the even more celebrated *ch'ai* ware, not yet identified with certainty, which from the native descriptions seems to have been of paper thinness with a glassy glaze resembling the colour of the sky after rain.

YING CH'ING WARE

It is possible that the *ying ch'ing* type (*Pl. 75*) may represent some form of *Ch'ai* ware, for *ying ch'ing* forms often come near to those of the T'ang era and in other respects the description seems to fit fairly closely.

With the Sung dynasty itself we arrive at a period when, from the point of view of form, the potters of no other nation at any time or period have been able to produce anything of comparable quality. Almost all the types have porcelain or at any rate stoneware bodies, while the glazes are high-fired felspathic compositions, extremely lovely both in colour and in quality. The architectural quality of many of the forms is emphasized by their beauty of proportion, while in details of construction such as handle or spout there is always a complete sense of fitness without the loss of any individuality. In decoration, where it is used, sureness of touch and rightness of taste are almost always present in a high degree. Of the many factories the highest class are represented by the *Ju, Ko* and *Kuan* wares, with the *Chün* following close behind.

JU WARE

There has always been considerable dispute as to the exact nature of *Ju* ware, and for a time it was thought that it was of the type of the *ying ch'ing* family, described above, with clear bluish glaze. But it is now fairly generally accepted that it is a ware with a buff body of porcellanous type, with a splayed foot-rim, derived from metal-forms, a thick greenish-blue glaze, as a rule crackled, the foot covered with glaze with a few small oval spur-marks. The pieces of this type are exceedingly rare, as indeed it is likely that they would be from a small kiln, producing in the precincts of the palace at K'ai-fēng fu things destined for Imperial use only.

KO AND KUAN WARE

The *Ko* and *Kuan* ware, both celebrated for their high quality, are extremely difficult to distinguish and it is, perhaps, better to treat them as of one family. They are both made of a fine dark grey body, often approaching the colour of rusty iron, while their glaze is unctuous, crackled, and varies in tone from a bluish-green to a soft white. The crackle on *ko*, which was the product of the elder of the two brothers Chang who worked at Lung chüan, seems to have been more regular than that on *Kuan* ware. As regards the glaze, that of the *Ko* seems to have a less glassy appearance than that of the *Kuan*, while small bubbles are frequently seen in the depth of the material. The spurs, which are underneath the foot, may take on the appearance of small seeds (*Pl.* 77).

CHÜN WARE

Chün ware is in some ways the most beautiful of all these from the wide variety of its colouring. The kiln was at Chün Chou in the province of Honan. The forms of the pieces are of domestic shape, flower-pots, drinking-bowls, wine-holders, etc. The paste is of two varieties, a rougher family varying in tone from greyish-yellow to reddish-buff (*sha t'ai*) and a close porcellanous type of a grey colour (*tz'u t'ai*). In the first class the glaze does not usually cover the body down to the foot and the colour, as a rule of some shade of soft blue, is often varied by splashes of a different shade, the commonest being a reddish-purple. In the higher class the glaze flows flush to the rim and the colour, of soft blue, purple, cherry-red, or olive-green, is of one tone though often shot with slight variations or varied by small worm-like veinings. The firing of these glazes took place at a very high temperature, but the potter was still able to control the extra modicum of iron or copper oxide with which he made his splash of a different shade (*Pl.* 76a).

CELADON

The largest and perhaps the best-known group of Sung wares is probably that with the grey-green glaze called 'celadon'. This type was produced in many places, but notably at Lung-chüan in the province of Chekiang. The glaze itself, varying considerably in colour and texture, obtains its pigment from iron, while the body of a grey close quality is easily recognizable by the bright red it turns when exposed to the fire (*Pl.* 73a). Among the many types made at Lung-chüan is one with a particularly beautiful light bluish-green glaze made by the brothers Chang who worked at the Han-liu hill; this variety is often known by the Japanese term for it, *kinuta*. A different type with dark olive glaze and floral designs carved under the glaze is associated with the North of China (*Pl.* 72).

TING WARE

The beautiful creamy-white ware known as *Ting* was made at Ting chou in the province of Chih-li; other varieties have been found in different parts of the country and it seems likely that there were many local products. The main group consists of ware with a greyish porcelain body covered with a white glaze, smooth in appearance with a few yellowish drops. The finest variety is known as *pai* (white) *Ting* (*Pls.* 78 and 79), a coarser sort being classified as *tu* (earthy) *Ting*. Exquisitely drawn floral sprays are engraved in the paste, while a more elaborate type has impressed designs of a more complicated nature. An allied ware found on the site of the town of Kulü-hsien, destroyed by flood in 1108 A.D., has a similar body, but a transparent glaze over a white slip (*Pl.* 82*a*). This glaze is often flushed with warm brown or grey discoloration. A further type with buff body and evenly crackled matt surface is associated with the Kiangnan district.

TZ'Ŭ CHOU WARE

From wares with a white glaze it is only a short step to the *Tz'ŭ chou* wares with their painted and engraved decoration, made at Tz'ŭ chou in Southern Chih-li. The body is of a dark buff-grey colour and the main group consists of pieces with designs painted in browns of various shades over a white slip under a clear glaze (*Pl.* 81). Variants of this type have the designs painted in red and green, while towards the close of the dynasty, a clear turquoise or green glaze is sometimes used over the brown decoration. Other types of design include pieces with patterns incised through the slip (*Pl.* 80*b*) and those in which the glaze is cut away to leave the biscuit as a contrasting ground colour (*Pl.* 83*b*). The kilns have a long history dating from pre-T'ang times and are still working with the same clay and types of decoration. It is consequently extremely difficult to be certain of the dating of Tz'ŭ chou pieces.

CHIEN WARE

The most typical product of the Chien kilns in the province of Fukien was the tea-bowl. The body at the original kilns was dark brown or grey in colour, but with the popularity of the ware other potteries began to make it, and a well-defined group found mainly in Honan has a light-buff body of a gritty nature. The colour of the glaze is always dark with brown the predominant tone and derives from iron, but a great variety of streaks and splashes are produced by the use of metallic oxides and the general effect is very varied. Arbitrary names have been applied to these to distinguish them, such as 'partridge pattern', 'hare's fur', the *temmoku* of the Japanese, 'oil-spot' and many others. The tea-bowls are often very beautiful in shape, with a refined conical form with tapering sides. In the most elaborate types motives are introduced into the pattern of the glaze by means of stencils (*Pl.* 84).

Sung Dynasty

Porcelain, as it is known to Europeans, did not come into existence in China much before the Ming dynasty (1368–1644 A.D.), but a large proportion of the Sung wares are true porcelain and a few of the T'ang pieces come very close to it, while as early as the third or fourth century A.D. the so-called 'proto-porcelain', referred to above, contained kaolin, the specific ingredient, which is the characteristic of 'true' porcelain, in its composition. In Europe we know it only as a translucent substance of a vitreous nature, but this is a very narrow definition of porcelain and if we consider the actual difference between earthenware and porcelain, which is that in the latter the two elements, the body and the glaze, become fused into a single substance capable of transmitting light, we see that the greater part of the Sung wares might be classified as porcelain. It is only within recent years that Sung ceramic art has really entered the comprehension of the Western world. Its qualities have had their immediate effect and it is safe to say that without the examples of the Sung potters before them none of the better-known of our modern studio-artists would have been able to produce what they have; even if we are unable to put their achievements with satisfaction beside those of the Chinese potters, we can at least realize that the influence of those Chinese potters has been a potent force in the development of one of the most healthy branches of modern art.

SUNG PAINTING

Wang Wei was the first poet-painter: in the Sung period and later almost all artists moved in literary circles and their interests were increasingly intellectual. Under the influence of Zen or contemplative Buddhism, their ideal, at least, was to live the life of a hermit in scenery of grand desolation. The period is divided into two halves by the invasion of the Tartars who seized the capital K'ai-fēng fu in 1125 and took prisoner the whole imperial family and the court. The northern part of the country was permanently lost and a new capital was established at Hang-chow in Chekiang. The earlier period is known as the Northern Sung and the later as the Southern Sung period.

The Northern Sung period is marked by the development of a landscape school which is the greatest achievement of Chinese art. Its course is broken at the end by the abortive attempt of the painter-emperor Hui Tsung to induce his Academy painters to study natural objects instead of imitating only the work of earlier artists. This style in its turn gives way after the political upheaval to a romantic school of landscape painting which reflects the desire of the exiled artists to forget their troubles in a communion with nature in its grandest aspects. An art of escape thus succeeds an art of reality.

169

Sung Dynasty

Landscape is the principal theme of Sung painting, and in its treatment there already begins to appear that divergence of two ways which were afterwards to be known as the Northern and Southern Schools. This terminology, which was apparently first used in the sixteenth century, has nothing to do with a geographical division, nor with the two epochs of Northern and Southern Sung; it is simply a terminology borrowed from a schism in the Zen Buddhist sect. The names themselves are no more significant than are those of Guelf and Ghibelline or Whig and Tory. The Southern School, which claimed descent from Wang Wei and whose greatest period was under the Northern Sung, is certainly the purer tradition. Like all who seek the end of contemplation, absorption in the absolute, they were purely intellectual in their means. Escape from the stream of phenomenal existence can only be by re-adjustment of values. The artist seeks to represent only what is essential in landscape, discarding all trivial and accidental effects. The result is a school of lofty and severe landscape painting such as the Western world has never known. There may not seem much difference to our eyes between such paintings as those of Tung Yüan, Fan K'uan or the other great Southern School painters (*e.g. Pl.* 64) and the more romantic, emotional art of Ma Yüan (*Pl.* 70) and Hsia Kuei (*Pls.* 68 and 69). But the Chinese have always tended to reject this method of allusive effect and association of landscape with human emotion which is characteristic of the work of the latter. It raises in us sympathy, humility and longing when we see these pictures of sages in their sublime natural surroundings (*Pls.* 65 and 66). What the Southern School artist seeks to do is to set down the object of contemplation in its whole reality and to express in the line the human means of approach to it, so that there can be no secondary interest and nothing superfluous in his painting. It is a dislike of the 'impurity' of their purpose that makes him intolerant of the Northern School. It would be impossible to put into words what he has set down in ink or wash, or to describe his paintings without entirely missing their point. Where there must be such stringent economy of means, there is no half-way place; a painting in this style either fails or succeeds. We may find the romantic Northern School easier to appreciate because it is not so far removed from what we find in Western painting. Difference of technique is not such an obstacle to understanding as difference of purpose. All Western landscape painting is romantic and its purpose is escape: it is therefore unreal. Chinese landscape painting in the Southern School style is something different and quite new to us. It requires not only loftiness of style but purity of life and true thought of the artist, as well as sensibility and skill in execution. Later on the Southern School was content with achievement on a lower plane though it preserved the technique and conception of painting of its first masters.

Sung landscape art thus passes beyond anything that we have yet experienced in Europe. It was able to do so owing to the existence of a cultured, unworldly society, inspired by common sympathies and informed with a common theory of art and life. Literary and philosophical criticism and exposition, for instance by the eleventh century painter Kuo Hsi, kept pace with the work of the artists.

Though Buddhism no longer occupied the central position that it did under T'ang there were still great painters of Buddhist subjects under Sung. The style of Wu Tao-tzŭ was still practised, and in addition, in the eleventh century, a new style was introduced by the great painter Li Lung-mien (1040–1106). He was a painter rather than a thinker and he had great respect for the models of antiquity which he copied. But, judging from the paintings attributed to him, or known from copies, his own style seems to have been severely linear (*Pl.* 61). When he painted in full colour he seems still to have used tone to accentuate his use of line, if we may judge of his Arhat painting from the set of paintings ordered in 1178 from two artists called Chou Chi-ch'ang and Lin T'ing-kuei and now preserved in Japan and in Boston (*Pl.* 67). In character his line was firm and precise rather than free and sweeping, but he was very successful in giving body and weight to his figures, which are monumental in scale.

Hui Tsung's injunction to the painters to study nature has already been mentioned. He reformed the Painters' Academy in order to raise painting to the same rank as literature. He put his large collection of old masters at their disposal and then told them to study natural objects and still-life.

The still-life paintings of this school, such as the 'Bird on the Bough' in the Eumorfopoulos collection, are intensely conceived. They are far from being purely decorative and yet they are not purely artificial arrangements made as exercises in painting. Once again in this naturalistic painting we find the attitude of the artist influenced by Zen thought.

6I. WANG MO (VIMALAKIRTI) WITH ATTENDANT APSARA
Attributed to LI LUNG-MIEN (*b. c. 1040 ; d. c. 1106*)

Hanging picture : ink on silk
Size : 35·5″ × 20·375″

MARQUIS KURODA NAGANARI, TOKYO

The attribution to Li Lung-mien is traditional in Japan where this is one of the most famous Chinese paintings. Li Lung-mien has been described as the last 'prose-painter' of China. He is said not to have used silk except when copying an old picture, but the present example seems to have all the qualities that would be expected from his outline painting. He was smitten with rheumatism in the arm and retired in 1100. He first painted horses, of which type the best example surviving is the roll of *Five Horses* lately in the possession of the Chinese Imperial Family, but now in Japan. Later, after the departure of a friend in the Imperial Stable, he took to Buddhist painting.

Reference : Tajima, *Selected Relics,* vol. viii.

62. QUARRELLING BIRDS
By HUI TSUNG (*b. 1082; d. 1135*)

Hanging picture in ink on paper

PRIVATE COLLECTION, SHANGHAI

Hui Tsung is without doubt the most skilful painter who has ever occupied a throne. Succeeding unexpectedly at the age of nineteen, he
was better suited to be a patron than an emperor. The paintings by
which he is best known are of birds and flowers minutely painted, of
which there is a number of famous examples in Japan. These bear his
signature or mark (which occurs at the top of the present picture, on
the left)—a character calligraphically written which has never been
satisfactorily explained. One or two also have inscriptions in his characteristic hand. In a famous edict Hui Tsung enjoined the Academy
painters to avoid imitation and to study nature. This is said to have been
issued under the influence of his progressive minister, Ts'ai Chin, and
to have been of short-lived effect. Hui Tsung's capital fell to the Tartars
in 1126, and he ended his life in captivity ten years later.

The present picture conveys a sense of space and movement which is
wanting in the tight realistic paintings of birds with which Hui Tsung's
name is generally associated. It is possible that he outgrew this tight
style (represented by pictures of birds, reproduced in the *Kokka*, Nos.
105, 386 and 472) and developed a freer style to be seen here and in
some landscapes preserved in China.

Reference : Tōsō gen min meigwa taikan.

63. LADY AT A DRESSING TABLE
By Su Han-ch'ēn (*about 1115–1170*)

Fan-shaped painting on silk in colours, mounted as an album leaf
Size: ·252 m. × ·267 m. (9·875″ × 10·5″)

MUSEUM OF FINE ARTS, BOSTON

The signature, which is partly cut away, appears on the lower left side of the painting. Su Han-ch'ēn was a member of the Academy and the painting is a good example of the rather tight meticulous style of its members. At the same time it is a strong, simple composition and the scene is sincerely felt, which saves it from any preciosity. Su Han-ch'ēn also painted a pair of large pictures of pedlars with children, in the Peking Palace collection, and is said also to have executed Buddhist frescoes.

Reference: Tomita, *Portfolio*, pl. 74.

64. LANDSCAPE WITH BUFFALOES
By CHIANG KUAN-TAO (c. 1200)

Scroll painting in ink on paper
Size : ·32 m. × 2·63 m. (12·6″ × 103·5″)
Detail : ·32 m. × ·60 m. (12·6″ × 23·7″)

METROPOLITAN MUSEUM, NEW YORK

This long scroll is a fine example of the Southern school during the Sung period. Very few paintings of this school and quality have ever left China. 'Chiang Kuan-tao (or more correctly Chiang Ts'an) followed the styles of Tung Yüan and Chü Jan, but excelled them in freedom of touch' [Waley]. The subject of buffaloes disporting themselves is a favourite one, but in fertility of invention and freshness the present example is among the finest. The landscape behind is severely classical in feeling though painted in broad washes.

Reference : Siren, *Chinese Paintings in American Collections*, pl. 111.

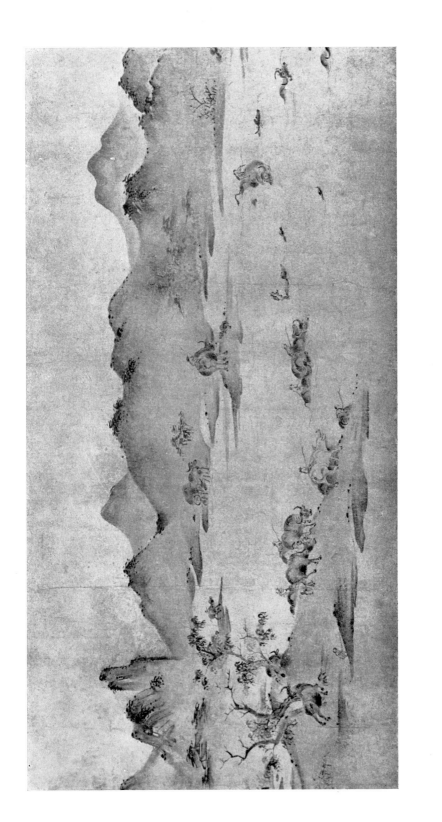

65 & 66. 'AUTUMN' AND 'WINTER'

A pair of landscapes. Painter unknown; 12th century

Hanging pictures in light colours on silk
Size: Each 49·875" × 21·5"

KONCHI-IN TEMPLE, KYOTO

This famous pair of landscapes has been in Japan since the fourteenth century when they were owned by the Shogun Ashikaga Yoshimitsu (1368–91). They bear the seals of two previous Chinese owners. They are traditionally ascribed to Hui Tsung and with them are preserved certificates by the famous Japanese artists No-ami, Kano Tannyu and Yasunobu. Nevertheless, in view of their completely different style from the rather tightly executed album pictures of birds and flowers with genuine signatures and inscriptions by Hui Tsung, modern scholars are unanimous in attributing them to some unknown master of the Southern Sung school. The old attribution may simply be taken as a tribute to the fine quality of these paintings, though Mr Waley suggests that they may be the product of Hui Tsung's earliest years when he was under the conservative influence of his brother-in-law, Wang Shēn, and his cousin, Chao Ta-nien, both distinguished painters. Stylistically, however, they seem to have affinities with the work of the Southern Sung artists of the Northern School.

References: Shimbi Taikwan, No. ii. Toyo Bijutsu Taikwan, vol. viii. Kokka, No. 155.

65 & 66. 'AUTUMN' AND 'WINTER'

A pair of landscapes. Painter unknown; 12th century

Hanging pictures in light colours on silk
Size: Each 49·875" × 21·5"

KONCHI-IN TEMPLE, KYOTO

67. TARTAR MAKING OFFERINGS TO ARHATS IN A BAMBOO GROVE

By LIN T'ING-KUEI (*fl. c. 1160–1180*)

Full colours on silk

Size: *1·115 m. × 0·531 m. (43·9″ × 20·875″)*

MUSEUM OF FINE ARTS, BOSTON

This painting forms part of a set of one hundred pictures representing the five hundred Arhats, of which eighty-two are still preserved in the Daitokuji temple, Kyoto, while ten are in the Museum of Fine Arts, Boston. They are known to have been executed by two painters called Chou Chi-ch'ang and Lin T'ing-kuei in the years 1178 onwards, for the Hui-an-yüan, a monastery at Ming-chou (modern Ning-po) in Chekiang. It was from this neighbourhood that many Chinese paintings found their way to Japan as the cities of Chekiang were thronged by Japanese merchants. This set of Arhats was taken to Japan in the thirteenth century. The artists are not otherwise known, but the series is superbly conceived and almost all the paintings have a truly monumental quality. Their realistic treatment may be an echo of the style of Arhat painting originated by Li Lung-mien.

References: O. Siren, *Chinese Paintings in American Collections*, pl. 62. Tomita, *Portfolio*, pl. 80.

68. TEN THOUSAND LI DOWN THE RIVER
By HSIA KUEI (*c. 1180–c. 1230*)

Detail from a handscroll in ink, on silk
Size: Length, 34' 8". Width 9·875"
Length of detail shown: 20·5"

PEKING PALACE MUSEUM

This long scroll is typical of this form of Chinese painting at its best. The strong cursive style carries one on from point to point and the variety of the treatment of water and rocks prevents one ever tiring of it. The treatment of the composition is extremely clever. Note for instance how on the right of the detail reproduced the water seems to swirl round the corner straight towards the spectator. The trees in the background to the left are washed in in a manner highly typical of Hsia Kuei's brushwork. The painting gives an epitome of the course of a river from a rushing torrent to a broad calm expanse. Water is the theme; water moving in accordance with its own laws and following its own life.

Reference: Published in full, from zinc blocks, in book form by the Peking Palace Museum.

Sung Dynasty

69a. SHIP IN THE RAIN
By HSIA KUEI (*c. 1180–c. 1230*)

Fan-shaped album leaf; ink and light colour on silk
Size: 23·9 cm. × 25·1 cm. (9·375″ × 9·875″)

MUSEUM OF FINE ARTS, BOSTON

The fan shape was the one most ordinarily favoured by the Chinese artists for small paintings. This example shows Hsia Kuei in a typical mood, painting wind over water. As the poem on the opposite leaf shows, the idea was that the ship was borne on by the same wind that beat on the cliff and through the trees, thereby uniting them in a fellowship. The title should perhaps be just *Wind and Rain*.

References: Tomita, *Portfolio*, pl. 85. *Kokka*, No. 255. *Chinese Paintings in American Collections*, pl. 14.

69b. TWO LINES FROM A POEM BY SU SHIH (1036–1101)
Written by the EMPEROR HSIAO TSUNG (*1127–1194*)

Fan-shaped album leaf. Ink on silk
Size: 23·9 cm. × 25·1 cm. (9·375″ × 9·875″)

MUSEUM OF FINE ARTS, BOSTON

The poem has been rendered:

'The wind beating against the cliffs all day,
Wafts the boats on.'

These two leaves faced one another in a famous album that is known by the name of a great connoisseur of the early nineteenth century Yüan-Yüan (1764–1849). During a journey on the Yangtze it fell in the water and traces of this mishap can be seen on both leaves.

References: Tomita, *Portfolio*, pl. 86. *Kokka*, No. 255.

平生慣足連江雨

盡日舟行摩岸風

7O. BARE WILLOWS AND DISTANT MOUNTAINS
By MA YÜAN (*fl. c. 1190–c. 1225*)

Ink and light colour on silk : fan-shaped
Size : 23·8 cm. × 24·2 cm. (9·4″ × 9·6″)

MUSEUM OF FINE ARTS, BOSTON

This small painting is a marvellous example of the Chinese use of tone in ink painting. It is also an excellent composition whose very simplicity gives it a more memorable quality. No doubt the two trees in the foreground are disproportionate to the small figure between them, but this may be taken as an allegory of the place of man in nature as conceived by the Chinese. The tree seen against the sky seems to express a cosmic purpose. The painter seems to have been able to combine simplicity with a rich romanticism. This was the peculiar gift of Ma Yüan, whose signature is mostly trimmed away, from the right side of the painting near the bottom.

References : Tomita, *Portfolio*, pl. 94. Siren, *Chinese Paintings in American Collections*, p'. 41. Binyon, *Spirit of Man in Asian Art*, pl. 26.

7I. A DRAGON

From the Scroll of the Nine Dragons executed in 1235
by CH'ĒN JUNG (*fl. c. 1235–1255*)

Scroll painting, ink on paper
Size : 46·3 cm. × 1096 cm. (18·25" × 35' 4·6")
Detail : 46·3 cm. × 77·2 cm. (18·25" × 30·4")

MUSEUM OF FINE ARTS, BOSTON

Ch'ēn Jung is the most famous Sung dragon-painter. In his day he was also highly esteemed as a poet and writer of prose. In addition he had a distinguished career as an administrator and rose to be Governor of P'u-t'ien in Fukien. Here he worked at land reclamation and in this as in all his other activities showed his vigour. This was evidently the first quality of his painting, but it no more than matches the subject of this scroll. At its end are inscribed a number of dragon stories which all go to show how to the Chinese the dragon is the most sublime conception, typifying no less than spiritual energy.

References : Boston Bulletin, 1917, pp. 67–73. Tomita, *Portfolio,* pls. 127–133.

72*a*. BOWL
Sung Dynasty (960–1279 A.D.)

Porcelain : Diameter 7″

VICTORIA AND ALBERT MUSEUM, LONDON

Carved with a free lotus-pattern in the paste under a celadon glaze of
olive tone, this bowl is a splendid example of the strong drawing of
the finest Sung patterns. It belongs in type to the so-called Northern
Celadon group.

72*b*. BOWL
Sung Dynasty (960–1279 A.D.)

Porcelain : Height 3·5″

VICTORIA AND ALBERT MUSEUM, LONDON

Covered with an olive-toned celadon glaze and decorated inside with a
scrolling leaf-pattern carved in the paste. The delicate proportions of
the conical form and the freely drawn pattern inside the bowl are both
admirable. The piece itself belongs to a large class of fine-quality celadons known as Northern Celadons. Many examples have been found
in Korea and certain pieces with grit attached to the foot-rim and a
body of greyish clay may well be Korean, but this piece is probably
to be classified as Chinese.

73a. BOWL
Sung Dynasty (960–1279 A.D.)

Porcelain Northern Celadon: Height 3·5″

MR H. OPPENHEIM, LONDON

Buff body, stained reddish colour where exposed, covered with a celadon glaze carved with a design of chrysanthemums in the paste.

73b. SAUCER DISH
Sung Dynasty (960–1279 A.D.)

Porcelain, Yüeh yao: Diameter 7″

MR H. OPPENHEIM, LONDON

Greyish body covered with an olive-celadon glaze, the exterior carved with a design of lotus petals, the interior engraved with two crowned phoenixes. Under the base piles of sand.

Fragments of this ware have been found in large quantities at Fostât outside Cairo, and have been identified as *Yüeh yao*, the *pi sē* or secret ware of the princes of Yüeh, made originally, no doubt, as a private ware in the ninth–tenth century, but later used for export purposes.

References: Burlington Magazine, July 1932. Ashton, *Trans. O.C.S.,* 1933–4.

74. VASE
Sung Dynasty (960–1279 A.D.)

Porcelain, Lung-chüan celadon : Height 12"

VICTORIA AND ALBERT MUSEUM, LONDON
(EUMORFOPOULOS COLLECTION)

This vase, exquisite in form, has the rare celadon glaze with iron spots in it, known in Japan as *tobi seiji*.

Sung Dynasty

75 EWER
Sung Dynasty (960–1279 A.D.)

Porcelain, ying ch'ing ware : Height 8″

VICTORIA AND ALBERT MUSEUM, LONDON

The beauty of form of this ewer is well set off by the fine bluish glaze of the *ying ch'ing* ware with its paper-like thinness and white paste.

Sung Dynasty

76a. BOTTLE
Sung Dynasty (960–1279 A.D.)

Porcellanous stoneware, Chün yao : Height 8"

VICTORIA AND ALBERT MUSEUM, LONDON

Admirable as ceramic form, the beauty of this vessel's proportion is still further enhanced by the lovely lavender glaze, suffused with purple.

76b. VASE
Perhaps Sung Dynasty (960–1279 A.D.)

Porcellanous stoneware : Height 9"

VICTORIA AND ALBERT MUSEUM, LONDON

This vase, exquisite in shape and proportion, is covered with an opalescent lavender-grey glaze, which bears some resemblance to *Chün yao*, but cannot by the body belong to that group. It is possibly a very early example of Kwang-tung stoneware.

77a. VASE
Sung Dynasty (960–1279 A.D.)

Porcelain, Ko yao : Height 5″ (without stand)

VICTORIA AND ALBERT MUSEUM, LONDON
(EUMORFOPOULOS COLLECTION)

With iron-black body, unctuous greenish-white glaze and broad reddish crackle, this vessel is a typical example of *Ko yao* of the Sung dynasty.

77b. BULB BOWL
Sung Dynasty (960–1279 A.D.)

Porcelain, Kuan yao : Height 3″

VICTORIA AND ALBERT MUSEUM, LONDON
(SALTING COLLECTION)

This bowl with an elephant-grey glaze, dark body and wide-meshed crackle, though a little unusual in colour, is otherwise a typical example of what is now accepted as *Kuan yao*. Underneath the base a mark, presumably indicating its inclusion in the Palace collections, has been ground away.

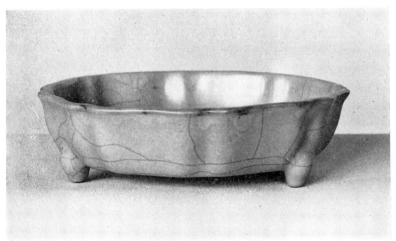

78. BOWL
Sung Dynasty (960–1279 A.D.)

Porcelain, Ting yao : Diameter 9″

MR H. OPPENHEIM, LONDON

Engraved with a design of lotus-plants drawn with that careless ease which often distinguishes the designs on this lovely class of porcelain.

79. DEEP DISH
Sung Dynasty (960–1279 A.D.)

Porcelain, Ting yao : Diameter 10″

MR H. OPPENHEIM, LONDON

The vitality of drawing and sense of decoration of the Sung potters is admirably shown in the tossing waves which fill half the field of the design.

80*a*. VASE
Sung Dynasty (960–1279 A.D.)

Porcelain, Ting type: Height 8"

VICTORIA AND ALBERT MUSEUM, LONDON

This vase is an outstanding example of ceramic form and ceramic ornament adapted to that form. The built-up body and the cut design are admirable elements in a particularly well-proportioned vase.

80*b*. BOWL
Sung Dynasty (960–1279 A.D.)

Stoneware, Tz'ŭ chou ware: Diameter 8"

VICTORIA AND ALBERT MUSEUM, LONDON

Transparent glaze over a white slip; buff body, with a band of ornament cut through the slip to the paste.

8I. VASE

Sung Dynasty (960–1279 A.D.)

Stoneware, Tz'ŭ chou ware : Height 14″

VICTORIA AND ALBERT MUSEUM, LONDON

This lovely vase is an outstanding example of the beauty of the free brush-work of the Sung potters.

82*a*. EWER
Sung Dynasty (960–1279 A.D.)

Porcellanous stoneware : Height 11″

VICTORIA AND ALBERT MUSEUM, LONDON

Admirable in form, with a creamy-white glaze, suffused with brown, this ewer belongs to a type largely found on the site of the city of Kü -lu hsien, submerged in 1108 A.D., and often known by that name.

82*b*. PILLOW
Sung Dynasty (960–1279 A.D.)

Stoneware, Tz'ŭ chou ware : Length 9″

VICTORIA AND ALBERT MUSEUM, LONDON

Painted in light brown with a design of two *bseru* holding leaves in their mouths.

83*a*. JAR
Sung Dynasty (960–1279 A.D.)

Stoneware, Tz'ŭ chou ware : Height 9″

VICTORIA AND ALBERT MUSEUM, LONDON

Dark brown glaze, buff body.

83*b*. JAR
Sung Dynasty (960–1279 A.D.)

Stoneware, Tz'ŭ chou ware : Height 14″

VICTORIA AND ALBERT MUSEUM, LONDON

Dark brown glaze with a band of floral ornament cut through to the buff body. Both these vases are admirable examples of a strong form and simple decoration in a utilitarian vessel.

84. BOTTLE

Sung Dynasty (960–1279 A.D.)

Stoneware, Chien yao : Height 11″

MR H. OPPENHEIM, LONDON

Brownish body with a blackish-green glaze stencilled with flower sprays in orange-brown.

85*a*. BOWL

Perhaps T'ang Dynasty (618–906 A.D.)

Glass: Height 11″

MRS WILFRED BUCKLEY, ENGLAND

There are no parallels to this lovely bowl, which both in form and decoration interpret so admirably the quality of its material, but it appears of considerable age and the strength and beauty of its conception urge its association with a period when Chinese art was at its most virile.

85*b*. BOWL

Perhaps Sung Dynasty (960–1279 A.D.)

Glass, painted in unfired pigment: Height 5″

ROHSSKAKABINET, GÖTEBORG

Early pieces of Chinese glass are rare and questions of dating are necessarily hazardous. The design painted on this bowl with its archaistic reminiscences of bronze patterns suggests the Sung dynasty when so much imitation of venerable pattern took place, but it is difficult to be more precise.

86. SILK WEAVING
Perhaps Sung Dynasty (960–1279 A.D.)

Width 7"

BRITISH MUSEUM, LONDON

The floral design is in white, green and yellow on a dark blue ground. The panel itself comes from the end of the celebrated Ku K'ai-chih scroll. Its proximity to the Sung seals combined with its broad spacing treatment of the design make it possible that this may be a Sung textile; it is certainly of a considerable age.

YÜAN DYNASTY

(1280–1368 A.D.)

The Yüan dynasty, which from the time of the Great Kublai Khan (1263–94) dominated China for almost a century, while it did not alter to any great extent the artistic ideals of the community, introduced by its cosmopolitan outlook and its wide commercial relations some new elements to China, which were to have considerable importance immediately and at a later date. Chief of these was the Mohammedan.

ARAB TRADE

During the centuries between the T'ang dynasty, when we first hear of the Arab sea trade with China, and the Yüan, this trade had been gradually growing. Arab settlements in China had increased in number and by the thirteenth century, when the size of the Chinese boats had become so large that they were able to sail direct to Aden without any transshipment of cargo at Calicut or Basra, the Sino-Arabian trade was in an extremely flourishing condition. Its chief effect on the applied arts of the period is visible in the very large quantity of export textiles made especially for the Mohammedan market, in particular for Egypt. These textiles, often with inscriptions in *naskhi* lettering, were re-exported to Europe and have been found in many European treasuries (*Pl.* 94); they seem to have been used also by the rich in the West, for when the tomb of Can Grande at Verona was opened within the last few years, he was found to be dressed in robes of Chinese brocaded silk. These weavings in which gold thread is largely employed are noted for the type of this thread which consists of gilt strips pasted flat on to a membrane, as opposed to the Western method of winding it round a core of a similar nature.

Kublai Khan favoured Lamaism as a suitable form of Buddhism for his soldiers, and the power of the Tibetan element had some effect on the sculpture of the date. Archbishop P'agśpa had a favourite called Aniko, a youth from Nepal, whose abilities as a sculptor were in great demand, and it is at this date that begin to appear the gilt-bronze figures of Nepalese type, which later became so common. Aniko was head of a department, which was concerned entirely with the production of Buddhist images of the so-called Indian type and also with the decoration of architecture and it is probably to the activities of this department that the fine reliefs on the Chu Yüan gateway outside Peking are due.[1]

[1] Bushell, *Chinese Art*, Bk. ¹, Pl. 24.

225

Yüan Dynasty

The Mongol domination had a somewhat curious effect on Chinese painting. To outward appearance the art flourished and court patronage was as freely extended as before. There was therefore no cultural break. We find a painter Chao Mēng-fu, who was actually a member of the Sung imperial family, in high favour at court. But some of the more independent artists like Ch'ien Hsüan declined to work for the barbarians, and it seems that this meant a loss of initiative to Chinese painting which ultimately left it so weak that it was not able to take full advantage of the return to a normal national life under the Ming dynasty. The Yüan court was as anxious to preserve Sung culture as it was to use Chinese methods of government. No one is more conservative than the *arrivé* and it was this influence which encouraged the natural conservatism of the painting schools. Already in the days of the Mongols, when China formed part of a great empire, the way was prepared for the complete closing of the door to any foreign influence or domestic change. The imitation of T'ang subjects did not bring a return of T'ang vitality.

But in the meantime the Sung tradition continued to produce great artists. The most typical of the period seem to be the 'Four Masters of Yüan', Huang Kung-wang, Wang Mēng, Ni Ts'an and Wu Chēn (*Pl.* 88), who represent the Southern School, rather than artists like Jēn Jēn-fa who painted the popular subject of the day, horses (*Pl.* 89). We are fortunate in this period in being able to judge the work of the greatest names by a comparatively large number of examples still known to exist. The great exception to this must be Chao Mēng-fu to whom so many paintings of horses are attributed, but who is known in the literary school mainly as a copyist of the old masters and an exponent of the literary style, painting in ink such subjects as 'Rocks and Bamboos'. Some paintings of the last sort attributed to him are preserved in China, but as he became the idol of the 'Literary Man's' school it is certain that some of these must be copies. Of the pictures of horses in Europe and America none has a really satisfactory title.

The 'Four Masters' are especially admired in China because of their characteristic of '*i*' or aloofness. They did not come to court but lived a life which ignored the new rulers.

There is little to distinguish the ceramics of the Yüan from those of the Sung dynasty, except that the former are as a rule of not quite so high a quality as the latter, but it seems likely that during this period one of the most important styles of decoration was introduced, that of painting in underglaze blue. Certain pieces of this ware found in tombs have been attributed to the Sung dynasty, but there is no certain proof of the date of any piece before the David vase dated 1352 A.D. This vase shows considerable ability and cannot have been one of the first pieces of blue and white produced, but for such quick learners as the Chinese only a few months would be necessary to acquire the methods of a new technique. The chief importance of this new style of decoration lies in the fact that underglaze blue requires a fine-grained porcelain for its painting and it is directly due to its introduction that the highest class of white kaolinic paste was developed, to act as a groundwork. It is possible that at Kublai's court, where many Persians were installed—his Chancellor of the Exchequer, whose paper currency was such a success, was a Persian—some specimens of Rayy or Sultanabad wares with underglaze blue painting were in use and that it was to emulate these that the Chinese potters started on their long career as 'blue and white' artists.

87. SQUIRREL AND PEACHES
By Ch'ien Hsüan (*b. 1235; d.c. 1290*)

Handscroll in delicate colour on paper
Size: 11·5″ × 22″

PEKING PALACE MUSEUM

Like Chao Mēng-fu, Ch'ien Hsüan was a native of Wu-hsing in Chekiang and lived most of his life under the Sung; but, unlike him, he did not adorn the Mongol court but went into retirement. He is best known from literary sources for his bird and flower paintings. He is said to have based his style on Chao Ch'ang and Chao Po-chü. This painting shows a rare sense of design, but is not so intensely felt as some of the Northern Sung flower paintings. It bears an inscription from the hand of the Emperor Ch'ien Lung in whose collection it was.

Reference: Ku Kung Shu Hua chi, No. xxvi.

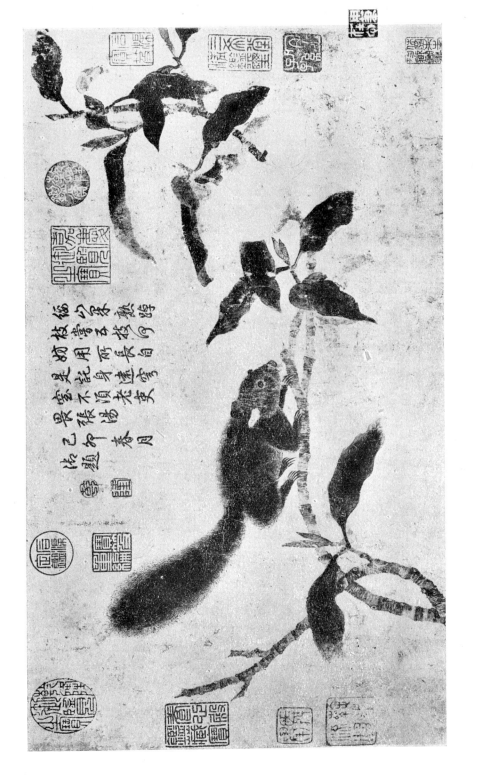

88. BAMBOO SHOOTS
By Wu Chēn (*b. 1280; d. 1354*)

Album painting : ink on silk
Size : *22·8 cm. × 22·5 cm. (8·75″ × 8·5″)*

BRITISH MUSEUM (EUMORFOPOULOS COLLECTION)

Wu Chēn, one of the Four Masters of the Yüan dynasty, was popularly known as the 'Priest of the Plum-blossom', and this painting is in fact signed 'Plum Blossom Taoist'. It comes from the album of the viceroy Tuan Fang in which the famous *Bird on the Bough* was also included.

Wu Chēn excelled in landscape, bamboos and trees. The bamboo was a subject of such importance to the Chinese artist that its study formed a special part of the art of painting comparable with figure painting or landscape. For this the idea of the bamboo as symbolic of Wisdom and Uprightness which was early current in China, was partly responsible. (See Petrucci's note on p. 262 of his edition of the *Mustard Seed Garden*.) In addition it is easy to see that it makes an admirable subject for the ink painting. It is said that Wu Chēn in his bamboo painting imitated the classic Sung master of this art, Wēn T'ung (*d.* 1079); by which it is probably intended that he was worthy of comparison with him, for his style seems to have been different in character, this difference being expressed by the epigram 'Wēn T'ung concealed his pictures under his bamboos: Wu Chēn concealed his bamboos under his picture'. From this we must understand that Wēn T'ung was realistic in his painting, while Wu Chēn was inclined to mannerisms. There are some fine paintings by Wu Chēn in the Peking Palace Museum.

References : Catalogue of the George Eumorfopoulos Collection, No. 4. *Chinese Paintings in English Collections*, pl. xviii (2).

89. FEEDING HORSES
By JĒN JĒN-FA *(14th century)*

Hanging picture : ink and light colours
Size : 21·5″ × 29·75″

VICTORIA AND ALBERT MUSEUM (EUMORFOPOULOS
COLLECTION)

Jēn Jēn-fa, often known as Jēn Yüeh-shan, was a native of Sungkiang.
He had a distinguished official career and rose to be assistant governor
of Eastern Chekiang. Like most of the Chekiang artists his works found
their way to Japan where several are still preserved. It is to be noted that
the seals on the present painting 'Jēn Tzü-ming' occur in exactly the
same form on a painting of a horse tethered to a post, in the collection
of Marquis Asano (reproduced Kokka, No. 403). Professor Siren considers this to be one of his finest surviving works. The present painting,
which is certainly no less fine, has also a signature 'The painting of
feeding horses by Yüeh-shan Tao-jēn'.

He was most famous for his paintings of horses, which he is said to
have painted 'after the best T'ang masters'. The Ch'ien Lung collection
contained a long roll by him representing 'dragon steeds' and a similar
picture (classified as a copy) dated 1314. This painting has this in
common with European painting, that it is addressed to a comparatively
unsophisticated public, the Mongol conquerors, who were glad of a
change from the difficult landscape paintings of the day. But it is by an
artist whose sympathies were rather with the latter style.

References: The George Eumorfopoulos Collection: Catalogue of the Chinese (etc.)
Paintings, No. 30, pl. xxiii (in colour). *Chinese Paintings in English Collections*, pl. xxx.

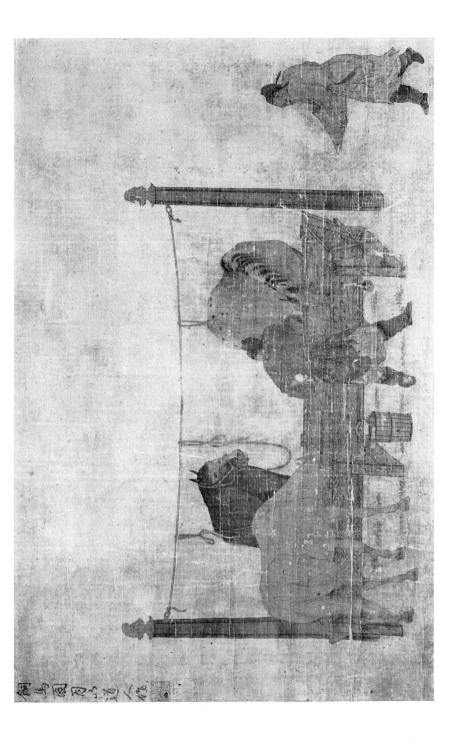

Yüan Dynasty

90. MOUNTAIN LANDSCAPE WITH A SAGE ON
A BRIDGE
Painter unknown : 14th century

Hanging picture, in ink, on silk
Size : 1·48 m. × 89 cm. (58·25″ × 47″)

MR H. OPPENHEIM

The picture bears an attribution to the well-known Sung artist Hsü Tao-ning (early eleventh century). But the execution is certainly of later date and this painting may be considered as a fine example of Yüan ink landscape painting. Technically it is connected with the style of the Northern Sung artists like Hsia Kuei: and this subject may actually be borrowed from one of the old masters, but the interest is not romantic. It is not so much in the subject as the brushwork. One cannot help feeling that the mountains are treated a little as an exercise: the painting definitely falls to the Southern school.

Reference : Chinese Paintings in English Collections, pl. xxv.

Yüan Dynasty

9I. LOTUS AND WAGTAILS

Attributed to WANG YÜAN (*14th century*)

Hanging painting. Full colours on silk
Size: 11·75″ × 14·33″

MARQUIS KURODA NAGANARI, TOKYO

Wang Yüan or Wang Jo-shui was a pupil of Chao Mēng-fu, the famous artist and statesman from the Academy who consented to work for the Mongol conquerors. Wang Yüan lived at Ch'ien-t'ang near Hangchow, a district much frequented by Japanese merchants. Consequently he is better known in Japan where this is considered one of his finest works. In bird-and-flower painting he is said to have imitated Huang Chüan of the tenth century. This picture depends for its charm on the contrasting textures of the ragged leaf and smooth flower, and on the elaborate balance of the composition. It is much more objectivized than are the Sung bird and animal paintings.

References: Shimbi Taikwan, xx, 17. *Toyo Bijutsu Taikwan*, vol. ix, pl. 106.

92. KUAN-YIN
Yüan Dynasty, dated 1282 A.D.

Wooden statue : Height 17″

METROPOLITAN MUSEUM, NEW YORK

The group of wooden statues of graceful proportions with flowing drapery which are the chief output of Buddhist sculpture of post-T'ang date centres round this little figure with its inscribed votive dedication. While some are probably rather earlier than this particular example, the end of the Sung dynasty can now be accepted as a middle date for the whole group. Artistically they show a softness and heaviness compared with earlier Buddhist sculpture, but the rhythmical flow of the drapery and the compassionate expression of the faces are often very beautiful.

93. IVORY RELIEF: A YAK
Perhaps Yüan Dynasty (1280–1368 A.D.)

Height 7·4″

M. ADOLPHE STOCLET, BRUSSELS

Ivories of an early date from China are exceedingly rare. There is no evidence for dating such a piece as this relief, but if we find some affinity between it and the paintings of Chao Mēng-fu, we may tentatively place it in the Yüan dynasty. Whatever its date, nothing can affect the beauty of its conception and execution.

94. BROCADED SILK TISSUE
Yüan Dynasty (1280–1368 A.D.)

Height 27″

MARIENKIRCHE, DANZIG

Woven in black silk and gold thread consisting of strips of gold pasted flat on to a membrane. The inscription on the wings of the parrots is in honour of En-Nasir, one of the titles of Mohammed Ibn Qalâun (1293–1341 A.D.) the Mamluk ruler of Egypt to whom the Arab chronicler Abu-el-Fida records the presentation of 700 pieces of silk with his title woven in by a Mongol Mission in 1323 A.D.

Yüan Dynasty

95. SILK DAMASK WITH DESIGN EMBODYING
THE CHARACTER 'SHOU'
13th–14th century A.D.

Pale blue and buff: Height 9″

VICTORIA AND ALBERT MUSEUM, LONDON

This damask belongs to a group, which has been attributed at various times to both China and the Near East. In this particular case the motive in the centre of the palmettes, which consists of the word Mohammed, has been split up in an arbitrary decorative manner, which would never have been countenanced by a Near Eastern designer.

Found at El-Azam, Egypt.

Yüan Dynasty

96a. BOWL

Probably Yüan Dynasty (1280–1368 A.D.)

Stoneware, Tz'ŭ chou ware: Height 8"

RUTHERSTON COLLECTION, ENGLAND

Painted with three fishes in two shades of brown on a creamy ground. Strong in form, the straightforward brushwork of the design achieves its effect by the simplest means and is admirably suited to the somewhat rustic quality of the piece.

96b. VASE

Yüan (1280–1368 A.D.) or early Ming

Stoneware, Tz'ŭ chou ware: Height 8"

MUSEUM OF FINE ARTS, BOSTON

Painted with a floral design in two shades of brown on a creamy ground.

MING DYNASTY REIGN MARKS AND DATES

洪武
年製

Hung Wu
1368–1398

大吉
新

Yung Lo
1403–1424

永樂
年製

Yung Lo
1403–1424

Chien Wān
1399–1402

Hung Hsi
1425

大明宣
德年製

Hsüan Tē
1426–1435

（篆書印章）

Hsüan Tē
1426–1435

大明成
化年製

Ch'eng Hua
1465–1487

Chēng T'ung
1436–1449

Ching T'ai
1450–1457

T'ien Shun
1457–1464

大明弘
治年製

Hung Chih
1488–1505

大明正
德年製

Chēng Tē
1506–1521

大明嘉
靖年製

Chia Ching
1522–1566

大明隆
慶年製

Lung Ch'ing
1567–1572

大明萬
曆年製

Wan Li
1573–1620

大明天
啟年製

T'ien Ch'i
1621–1627

崇禎
年製

Ch'ung Chēng
1628–1644

MING DYNASTY

(1368–1644 A.D.)

In the reaction from the cosmopolitan elements of the Yüan domination, Hung Wu (1368–1398 A.D.), the founder of the Ming dynasty, swept everything aside in favour of a return to the glories of the past. The effect of this on the arts was to further academic interests and for a time, at all events, this academic quality is very noticeable, particularly in the major arts. Ming sculpture is of little interest and, while the monumental figures in front of the tomb of Yung Lo (1403–1424 A.D.) are impressive, they entirely lack the vitality of the T'ang originals they are emulating, in the same way that the Ming tomb-figures lack the charm of their T'ang ancestors.

MING PAINTING

In painting, the Ming period, in its earlier part, showed a change of emphasis rather than a falling off from the Sung period. No doubt there is a weakening of conception even in the work of artists like Wu Wei, T'ang Yin or Lin Liang. They painted mainly birds and rushes, or flowers, and figures in ink alone or ink and light colours, such as the 'Geese and Reeds' in the British Museum by Lin Liang, or the phoenix by the same artist reproduced here (Pl. 100). In these paintings the interest is transferred from the subject to the brush-work. It should at once be pointed out that this means something rather different from what we mean in Europe. Brush-work in China implies not only line, but also tone—the subtle variations of tone in a picture, which is known in Japan, where this sort of style was much copied, as *Notan*, and which distinguish the work of the great masters. Excellence of brush-work then does not imply virtuosity but all that technical side of his work which makes an artist a great painter. Though, of course, the early Ming period had no monopoly of technical excellence, it is in this period perhaps that it reaches its highest point.

In the sixteenth century two tendencies, both detrimental to good painting, became clearly pronounced. In the first place the worldliness of the court demanded purely decorative paintings. These were executed in a light minute style, and colouring became brighter. This is the type of painting which is usually associated with the name of Ch'iu Ying (*fl.* 1522–60), of which countless later copies have found their way to Europe. He also seems to have painted in a more literary style. Apart from these figure subjects, there are paintings of birds and flowers in bright colours, or in ink and full colours, by artists like Lu Chih (1495–1576). The other tendency, which affected the more intellectual painters, was towards academic rigidity. This tendency came from the school which in the fifteenth century had produced such free and individual work from the hands of artists like Shēn Chou (*Pl.* 99), Wēn Chēng-ming and Tai Chin (*Pl.* 98). Dispensing with anything but the bare minimum of line they produced landscapes in ink which are wonderfully sensitive and suggestive. In the work of Tung Ch'i-ch'ang (*b.* 1554; *d.* 1636), however, the regard for the models of antiquity became all-powerful. He was first and foremost a literary man and a collector of old masters. When he and his fellows took up the brush they did not make an original composition, but chose some work by one of the great Sung or Yüan masters of the Southern School as their model. It was like playing over a piece by Bach or, perhaps, still more like arranging it for a modern orchestra—except that in this case they chose a more limited medium than the original.

Such virtuosity has never been known in European painting, but it is easy to understand that for those practising it, it would be a dogma that the style of different old masters must not be mixed. In literary circles this soon became accepted as the only polite style of painting. For anyone who has the key to this world of intellectual painters there is much pleasure of a rare kind to be gained, but it has led to painting in China falling entirely into the hands of a highly educated literary class, with consequent impoverishment of the nation's life and of its painting.

The most important developments of the Ming dynasty are certainly in the realm of ceramics, where a completely new style arose, a style in which the decorative element as opposed to the architectural, if one may so describe concentration on form and glaze, was emphasized.

MING CERAMICS

The removal of the capital to Nanking in the South and the rise to fame of the factory of Ching-tē Chēn, a site well provided with ample deposits of the finest white clay, were factors in the evolution of this change. While the simple monochromes of the Sung period continued to be made, supplemented in many cases by the more brilliant yellow, aubergine or turquoise of the new palette, the principal output of the factories was concerned with painting in underglaze blue or copper-red or in overglaze enamels. With the successful production of these decorative wares, porcelain, as it is known to Europeans, came into its kingdom and it is by this class of Chinese porcelain that the art has been known in the West for centuries. Of the types surviving from the Sung dynasty the celadon and *Tz'ŭ chou* factories were the only two to flourish to any considerable extent. The latter altered its types very little, but the former, changing its site from Lung-chüan to Ch'u chou, tends to a glaze less unctuous and more watery in colour, though forms and body remain much as before (*Pl.* 104). The many rich self-coloured glazes used by the Ming potters were often engraved with elaborate designs in the paste under the glaze, the same method being used on the exquisite plain white bowls (for which the reign of Yung Lo was celebrated), which are one of the most beautiful products of the epoch; this type of decoration is known as *an hua* (secret). Decoration in white slip over the glaze was also used with these self-colours.

Under the earlier reigns of the Ming dynasty the blue used in the painting of the underglaze blue and white seems to have been of a pale shade, dotted with a darker tone often speckled with black (*Pl.* 107a). The description given in native sources as heaped or piled is a very accurate one. The finest cobalt, known as *su-ni-p'o* or *hui hui ch'ing* (Mohammedan blue), was imported, probably from Persia, and being expensive, was usually mixed with the coarser native variety, with which it did not always combine very well. The white glaze in these earlier reigns is of a fatty quality often with a close orange-peel surface, and sometimes pitted with small holes. The paste of the body is as a rule burnt a pinkish-red at the edges. The custom of marking the pieces under the foot in blue with the name of the period, as a rule in a double ring or square, began to be widely used at this date, though it is not always possible to accept the mark as evidence of the period, as in the later reigns the potters often put on the mark of an earlier and celebrated reign in emulation of their skilful forebears. The most prized period is that of the Emperor Hsüan Tē (1426–1435 A.D.), but the same types were being made considerably earlier, a group of pieces in the Seraglio Museum at Constantinople showing the types well (*Pl.* 105). The larger vessels are distinguished by the bold qualities of the drawing with splashes of floral decoration with distinctive spiked leaves and splendid dragons, wave decorations or phoenixes (*Pl.* 105). In all this family the close connection between the patterns on porcelain and those on textiles is very noticeable. In the smaller and more finely painted objects, a deliciously sensitive line is apparent (*Pl.* 107a), which the later imitations were never able to achieve. To this reign also belong the famous stem-cups decorated with fishes or peaches in rich underglaze copper-red. This fresh red (*hsien hung*) was also used as a self-colour glaze on such objects as saucer-dishes and brushpots. The second great period of the Ming underglaze blue was that of Ch'ēng Hua (1465–1487 A.D.). Here the blue is as a rule of a paler tone without any of the heavy piled appearance of the earlier date, while the designs, planned on a less robust scale, rely for their appeal on delicacy of detail and admirable spacing (*Pl.* 107*b*). Under the reign of Chēng Tē (1506–1521 A.D.) a particularly strong wave of Mohammedan influence seems to have had vogue and many pieces show this effect not merely in the style of the motives, but by the introduction of inscriptions in Arabic.

In the sixteenth century the style of decoration becomes more elaborate and detailed and the designs are often treated in a very pictorial way. While under Chia Ching (1522–1566 A.D.) the blue used was mainly of a very rich violet hue (*Pl.* 111*a*), under Wan Li (1573–1619 A.D.) a delightful silvery tone was much employed, particularly on a large class of almost transparent dishes with sketchily drawn landscapes or bird and flower designs, much exported to the West (*Pl.* 114*a*). The groups of fragments of blue and white found at Fostât, the site of the old city of Cairo, have provided a long and interesting series of export types, which tend to confirm the conclusion of some of the dates now usually accepted; other sources of confirmation are the fragments from Aidhab and Karakhoto, both sites with *termini ad quos*, and a more recently investigated source of information is that of dated Persian MSS.

POLYCHROME ENAMELLED PORCELAIN

Porcelain of the Ming dynasty decorated in coloured enamels belongs to two types. The first consists of a large group with designs engraved, pierced or modelled in relief. The enamel is painted on the biscuit in small fields—it is in reality a lead silicate glaze treated in an enamel technique—separated as a rule by small raised fillets outlining the design. The main colours used were yellow, aubergine, turquoise, dark blue and green, white being employed by means of a colourless glaze put over the biscuit. The colours were, as a rule, not all employed together and the class is known to the Chinese as *san ts'ai* (three coloured). A magnificent series of this family can be confidently dated in the fifteenth century (*Pl.* 108), but the type was made right to the end of the dynasty.

The second type consists of porcelain enamelled over a white glaze with what is in reality glass stained with metallic oxides, which being fired at a lower temperature than the porcelain itself can be used without damaging the surface at the second firing. The colours of green, aubergine, turquoise and yellow are supplemented by iron-red, and black, the latter low-fired pigments. With these enamels underglaze blue was often employed and the combination of several of these colours was known in China as *wu ts'ai* (five-coloured). In the fifteenth century the enamels show a tendency to opacity and a certain roughness of surface (*Pl.* 106), though on the finest pieces, such as those of the reign of Ch'eng Hua (*Pl.* 109), during which a celebrated type of wine-cup was produced, known from its decoration as a chicken cup, the utmost brilliance was obtained. The types of design differ very little at the various periods from those of the blue and white. A distinctive palette in which a bright turquoise is the outstanding colour was much in use from about 1475–1525, while in the mid-sixteenth century a rich opaque red is present in a large number of pieces. The vogue of dark underglaze blue used in combination with pale colours is a feature of Wan Li (*Pl.* 112).

MING TEXTILES

The textiles of the Ming dynasty are many and various. The designs are almost always naturalistic and the majority are floral in character. The skilful use of scrolling stems, the happy arrangements of different plants, show the Chinese genius for pattern at a very high level. Conspicuous among the species used are the flowers of the four seasons, the peony, the prunus, the lotus and the chrysanthemum, while others often seen are the mallow, the magnolia, the aster and the paulownia. Brilliance of colour and the lavish use of gold thread are features of both weaving and embroidery, as also of the silk tapestry, known as *k'o ssŭ*, at which the workers were such adepts (*Pl.* 116). This material was produced by the same methods as in the West, but silk only was employed, while the execution is of such miraculous quality that the finished panels often appear to be painted. Indeed, in certain cases, the details have been touched in with a brush, though this is usually assumed to indicate a late date. Velvet is another material at which the Chinese weaver excelled, cutting his pile with a very deep edge and plentifully filling the ground with gold thread.

CARPETS

Chinese carpets have never been much appreciated by the collector, perhaps because their loose knotting and somewhat shaggy pile compare very unfavourably with the high quality of their Near Eastern rivals (*Pl.* 141). But the cool blues and yellows of the Chinese carpets, offset by a brick-pink, are singularly attractive and the patterns with simple floral motives and medallions contained within a formal border of geometric design follow the best traditions of carpet designing, while, when the workers employed silk, they managed to avoid any of the more unpleasant effects of the Near Eastern specimens. Many of the Chinese carpets are of a small size and shaped pieces for use on furniture are common. Another curious type is the pillar-carpet, the design of which does not complete itself unless wrapped round a cylinder.

LACQUER

Lacquer, in particular the carved variety, known as *tiao ch'i*, was much made during the Ming dynasty, the main centre of the industry being Soochow (*Pl.* 118). Ming lacquer is heavy in weight and carved with elaborate designs of landscapes, figure or animal subjects, the lacquer having been built up in layers of different colour, the top layer being carved through to the lower to show the contrasting tint. Ming lacquer is, as a rule, marked in the same way as porcelain, though in the earlier reigns the mark is often incised just inside the rim or in some other obscure place. Some of the more elaborate pieces are encrusted with semi-precious stones and gilt metal mounts. Painted lacquer (*hua ch'i*) was also made extensively, some of the pieces with sprays of flowers in colours against a scarlet ground being extremely beautiful.

CLOISONNÉ

While a few of the Ming bronze figures have a certain sculptural quality, it is in quite a different sphere that the metal workers achieved their greatest success. This was in the making of enamelled ware known from the method of its technique as *cloisonné* (*Pl.* 117). Most authorities agree that the Chinese derived their knowledge of the enamelling craft from the West, while the Chinese name for the work, *fa lan*, is derived from Fo-lin, the old Chinese name for the Roman Empire, which is a corruption of πόλιν, contracted from εἰς τὴν πόλιν, just as is Istanbul. Cloisonné enamel is made by tracing a design on the ground of the vessel and soldering to the metal a tracing of gold wire following the outlines of this pattern. The cells thus formed are filled with powdered metallic enamels and the piece fired. The firing completed, an elaborate process of polishing down takes place, till the surface has reached a sufficient pitch of excellence. The palette of the Ming cloisonné is particularly rich, a splendid lapis blue, opaque turquoise, dull crimson and grass-green being the predominant tones. While many reigns were noted for their productions, the short period of Ching T'ai (1450–1457 A.D.) seems to have been particularly celebrated, but it must be realized that it is the commonest mark copied, and very few pieces with this reign mark on them can belong to that date.

97*a*. THE BRONZE ARMILLARY SPHERE FROM THE OBSERVATORY, PEKING
17th century

Built by Kublai Khan, the Peking observatory is the oldest in the world. The original instruments were erected in 1279 by Kuo Shou-ching, but in the year 1670 Père Verbiest replaced them with more easily workable examples, designed after the old models, but following Tycho Brahe's calculations. Regarded simply as works of art they have a simplicity and beauty of proportion which is extremely distinguished.

97*b*. THE TARTAR WALL, PEKING
15th century

98. BREAKING WAVES AND AUTUMN WINDS
By TAI CHIN *(15th century)*

Scroll painting in ink, on paper
Size : 11·129 m. × ·299 m. (36′ 1″ × 11·4″)
Detail : about 26″ × 11·4″

FREER GALLERY, WASHINGTON

Tai Chin was one of the most important artists of the early Ming period. He seems to have been versatile in style, but evidently his chief characeristics were rapidity and freedom of brushwork and originality. He seems to have shocked his more academic contemporaries but was really a devoted admirer of the great Southern Sung masters of landscape. He is one of the painters of the 'Chē School'. Mr Waley suggests that he inherited the technique but not the spirit of the Southern Sung romantic painters. This seems a fruitful suggestion. The strict economy of means is, however, foreign to the Northern school painters.

Reference : O. Siren, *Chinese Paintings in American Collections*, pl. 141.

99. POET GAZING AT THE MOON
By SHĒN CHOU (*1427–1509*)

Detail from a scroll painting : ink on paper
Size : 0·30 m. × 1·34 m. (11·9″ × 52·75″)

MUSEUM OF FINE ARTS, BOSTON

Shēn Chou, who was a poet as well as a painter, was one of the founders of the 'Wu School' at Soochow. He is considered as the best fifteenth century representative of the Southern School of landscape painting. He is said to have imitated Mi Fei, whose style is well known from his mannerism of painting in parallel horizontal strokes, even though no work of his is certainly known. The present picture, however, is Northern in its subject. But in it can be seen clear traces of the beginnings of the literary style. From all this it is clear that the distinction between Northern and Southern school is quite arbitrary. What people like Shēn Chou disliked in the Northern School was their posing and their rigidity. He was much more light-handed and light-spirited. In some of his paintings[1] he approaches near to the style of Sesshiu, the great Japanese artist, who visited China during his lifetime and was settled in Chekiang from 1467–9. He acquired a great reputation with the Chinese literati and it is possible that he was as much imitated as influenced by them.

Reference : O. Siren, *Chinese Paintings in American Collections*, pl. 164.

[1] cf. *Ku Kung Paintings*, xiii, 8.

IOO. PHOENIX

By LIN LIANG (*fl. c. 1500*)

Ink painting on silk
Size: 5' 4·9" × 3' 2"

SOKOKUJI TEMPLE, KYOTO

Lin Liang is one of the best artists of the early Ming period, in his ink pictures almost equalling the masters of the Sung period. The British Museum has a fine example of his work in the *Wild Geese by a Mountain Stream*. This is reproduced by Mr Binyon in *Painting in the Far East* (Pl. xxviii). A painting, rather similar to the present in composition, by Chien Hsüan (cf. *above*) is preserved in Japan. A comparison of the two paintings reveals the more individual and natural style of the Ming artist as against the more monumental and detached painting of Sung.

Reference: Shimbi Taikwan, vol. xix. Tōsō gen min meigwa taikan.

IOI. AN IMPERIAL SUMMONS

By Hsü LIN *(early 16th century)*

Hanging picture in ink, on silk

MR KUNIZO HARA, TOKYO

Hsü Lin was a favourite painter at the court of the Emperor Wu Tsung [Chēng Tē] (1506–22). Typical of the discursive narrative style of Ming painting, this painting, though painted in accordance with Sung technical methods, is much more objectivized. The artist has had an eye to his public and is conscious of the surface of his picture. He has tried by technical devices to give monumental scale and recession. He has succeeded, but the painting remains a rather uncomfortable *tour-de-force*.

Reference: Tōsō gen min meigwa taikan.

IO2. BIRDS AND LYCHEES
Artist unknown (16th century)

Scroll painting in full colours on silk
Size: Detail 34″ × 10·125″

BRITISH MUSEUM

This is an admirable example of later Ming flower painting in full colours and also of the treatment of such a subject in scroll form. These must so be painted that it is possible for the person unrolling them to stop at any point and have a satisfactory composition before him. Looking at a roll then is like reading a poem or listening to music: there may be a climax, but no part can be without interest and the theme must be maintained throughout. As well as the brushwork the observation displayed in the present picture is admirable.

Reference: Chinese Paintings in English Collections, pl. xlviii.

IO3. THE EMPEROR CH'ĒN SHU-PAO WITH HIS CONCUBINE

Attributed to CH'IU YING (*fl. 1522–60*)

Full colours on silk
Size: 5' 7" × 3' 4·75"

BRITISH MUSEUM

Although the colour has sunk a good deal this painting still remains magnificent in the richness and delicacy of its execution. The Emperor, who lived from 553 to 604 A.D. and was the last sovereign of the Ch'ēn dynasty, is seated in his chair, composing a poem: he has sent for his concubine to make music to aid his inspiration. Behind him is a six-fold screen with a landscape painted on it in ink and full colours. In the foreground are some fantastic bluish rocks such as the Chinese love to set up in their gardens. Unlike so many paintings of this style this picture does not bear any attribution to Ch'iu Ying. It is, however, much nearer to his style, so far as we can assess it, than most of them, and it has also the appearance of being an original work and not a copy. It comes from a well-known Japanese collection, that of Baron Kawasaki of Kobe, where it was attributed to Shēng Mou. It is, however, certainly of the Ming period.

Reference: British Museum Quarterly, vol. iv, No. 4.

IO4. VASE

Ming Dynasty (dated 1547)

Porcelain : Height 11·8"

VICTORIA AND ALBERT MUSEUM, LONDON

Celadon glaze of a watery green colour of the type made in the Ming dynasty after the removal of the kilns from Lung-chüan to Ch'u chou. The inscription runs: 'At the Pu-hsiao tomb in Wan Shan village, the pious lady, Madam K'ang I, having in answer to prayer obtained a son, brought a pair of flower-vases to the Hou-tēng shrine in front of the ancestral incense-burner and gave thanks, at the same time praying that the son so obtained might grow up to manhood.'

IO5. JAR
About 1400

Porcelain : Height 14″

VICTORIA AND ALBERT MUSEUM, LONDON
(EUMORFOPOULOS COLLECTION)

Painted in rich underglaze blue of uneven tone with piled-up depths and black spots, the drawing of the dragon shows the superb quality of much of this early Ming blue and white. The details of the leaf pattern on the sides may be compared with the David vase, dated 1352, while in general appearance it stands close to many of the pieces in the Seraglio, Constantinople. A similar jar appears in the front of the group in the Chinili Kiosque of the Mosque at Ardebil.

Reference : Sarre, *Persische Denkmäler*, pl. 52.

IO6. BOWL
Early 15th century

Porcelain : Height 3·6″

MRS WALTER SEDGWICK, LONDON

Enamelled in turquoise, yellow, green, aubergine and iron-red, this lovely bowl is closely related in quality of glaze and enamel to a bowl in the Sir Percival David Collection, dated in the ninth year of Hsüan Tê ʼ1435).

IO7*a*. HOT-WATER BOWL
Early 15th century

Porcelain : Diameter 6·4″

VICTORIA AND ALBERT MUSEUM, LONDON

This type of bowl with its hole in the base for pouring in the hot water and corking up is said to have been invented by a general for the use of his troops on campaign. The design in pale blue with blackish heaped-up spots is a charming example of Ming drawing.

IO7*b*. BOWL
Mark and period of Ch'ēng Hua (1465–1487 A.D.)

Porcelain : Height 2·25″

MR H. OPPENHEIM, LONDON

Painted with a bird on a branch in underglaze blue of a silvery tone. The blue used on Ch'ēng Hua porcelain has always been thought to be of a paler tone than that of previous reigns, owing to the failure of the import trade for a time, due to the disturbed state of affairs on the caravan route.

108*a*. CUP
15th century

Porcelain : Height 6·5"

MR H. OPPENHEIM, LONDON

Painted on the biscuit with turquoise, yellow, aubergine and colourless enamels on a dark blue ground. Both this cup and the vase (*Pl.* 108*b*.) are examples of the class known as *san ts'ai* or three-colour ware.

108*b*. VASE
15th century

Porcelain : Height 12"

VICTORIA AND ALBERT MUSEUM, LONDON

Painted on the biscuit with turquoise, yellow, aubergine and colourless enamels on a dark blue ground.

IO9. PILGRIM BOTTLE
Mark and reign of Ch'ēng Hua (1465–1487 A.D.)

Porcelain: Height 10″

VICTORIA AND ALBERT MUSEUM, LONDON

The polychrome enamelled porcelain of the Ch'ēng Hua period was justly celebrated, but very few pieces have survived. This bottle with enamels of scarlet, emerald-green, lavender and pale yellow over a design sketched in pale underglaze blue belongs to a group much imitated in the eighteenth century; but the quality of enamel, the individual and irregular drawing of the blue outline, combined with an unctuous and unequal surface of white, seem to indicate that this is a genuine example of the period.

IIO. SAUCER DISH
Mark and reign of Chēng Tē (1506–1521 A.D.)

Porcelain : Diameter 7"

VICTORIA AND ALBERT MUSEUM, LONDON
(EUMORFOPOULOS COLLECTION)

Painted in iron-red, green and turquoise enamels, the mark in iron-red
over the glaze. In spacing, freedom of drawing and quality of enamel,
this dish displays the highest form of Ming designing and technique.

III*a*. BOTTLE
Mark and period of Chia Ching (1522–1566 A.D.)

Porcelain : Height 13"

VICTORIA AND ALBERT MUSEUM, LONDON

Painted with a design of playing boys in rich violet-blue of a shade particularly associated with the reign of Chia Ching.

III*b*. JAR
Mark and period of Chia Ching (1522–1566 A.D.)

Porcelain : Height 9"

MR H. OPPENHEIM, LONDON

Painted with a design of fishes and waterweeds in underglaze blue and overglaze red, yellow, green and aubergine enamels, a typical example of the so-called *wu ts'ai* or five-colour decoration.

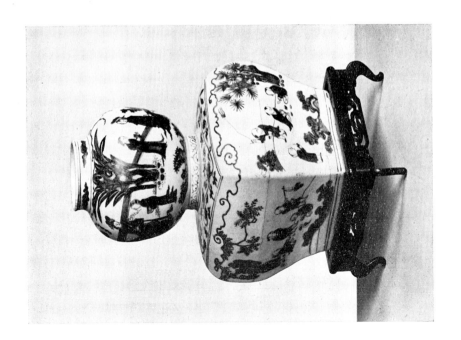

II2. FISH BOWL

Mark and reign of Wan Li (1573–1619 A.D.)

Porcelain : Diameter 32″

VICTORIA AND ALBERT MUSEUM, LONDON

Painted with a design of mandarin ducks and water plants in underglaze blue, and red, green and yellow overglaze enamels (*wu ts'ai*).

II3. JAR
Late Ming

Porcelain : Height 8"

VICTORIA AND ALBERT MUSEUM, LONDON

Painted in red and green overglaze enamels with a freely drawn spray of prunus. An example of the beauty sometimes achieved by factories in the provinces.

II4*a*. BOWL
Period of Wan Li (1573–1619 A.D.)

Porcelain: Height 4"

MR H. OPPENHEIM, LONDON

Painted with a free design of a bird on a rock in underglaze blue of a silvery tone. The thin potting, scalloped edge and delicate style of painting are typical of a large class of Wan Li blue and white.

II4*b*. SAUCER-DISH
Late Ming, about 1630–1640 A.D.

Porcelain: Diameter 8"

VICTORIA AND ALBERT MUSEUM, LONDON

Painted with a design of boys playing blind man's buff in underglaze blue of a violet tone. A delightful example of the freely drawn porcelain of the period after Wan Li and before K'ang Hsi, which had such an influence on seventeenth century Japanese porcelain.

II5. BRUSH-POT
Late Ming, about 1640

Porcelain : Height 7″

VICTORIA AND ALBERT MUSEUM, LONDON

Painted with the Eight Immortals in underglaze blue of a violet tone.

Ming Dynasty

116*a*. PANEL
Perhaps 15th century

Silk tapestry (k'o ssŭ) : Height 14"

HON. ROBERT AND MRS WOODS BLISS,
WASHINGTON, D. C.

This exquisitely rhythmical design of hō-hō birds amidst clouds is carried out in soft tones of buff, pink and blue. In particular, the treatment of the clouds shows that extraordinary sense of the fitness of
pattern to material in which the Chinese are so frequently vindicated.
While it is difficult to be at all precise about the dating of such pieces,
the drawing is undoubtedly of an early type and a comparison with
certain fifteenth century pieces of porcelain of the *wu ts'ai* group leads
one to suppose that this *k'o ssŭ* must be related in point of time to them.

116*b*. PANEL
16th–17th century

Silk tapestry (k'o ssŭ) : Width 12"

METROPOLITAN MUSEUM, NEW YORK

While certainly of the Ming dynasty, this charming design of a dragon-
horse has not quite the reserve and distinction of the panel above, and it
seems more likely that it belongs to the latter part of the period.

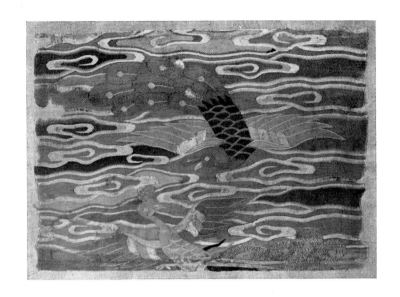

II7. VASE
Probably 15th century

Cloisonné enamel : Height 17"

This vase, of ancient bronze form, by its rich opaque colouring, in which red and dark blue predominate, is clearly of early date. Ming *cloisonné* is comparatively uncommon and differs in quality of colouring and enamel from its eighteenth-century successors by an extent very similar to that of enamelled porcelain.

II8. BOWL AND CUP-STAND

The cup-stand, mark and reign of Yung Lo (1403–1424 A.D.)
The bowl, mark and reign of Chia Ching (1522–1566 A.D.)

Cinnabar red lacquer
Height of cup-stand 5″ ; of bowl 4·3″

SIR PERCIVAL DAVID, LONDON

Both the cup and its stand belonged to the Emperor Ch'ien Lung. An inscription by him on the cup, dated 1778, records the fact that the original Yung Lo cup had been lost and that this Chia Ching substitute was used instead.

CH'ING DYNASTY REIGN MARKS AND DATES

大清順
治年製

Shun Chih, 1644–1661

大清康
熙年製

K'ang Hsi, 1662–1722

大清雍
正年製

Yung Chēng, 1723–1735

大清乾
隆年製

Ch'ien Lung, 1736–1795

嘉慶
年製

Chia Ch'ing, 1796–1821

大清道
光年製

Tao Kuang, 1821–1850

大清咸
豐年製

Hsien Fēng, 1851–1861

大清同
治年製

T'ung Chih, 1862–1873

大清光
緒年製

Kuang Hsü, 1874–1908

Hsüan T'ung,
1909–1912

洪憲
年製

Hung Hsien (1916)
(Yūan Shih-kai)

300

CH'ING DYNASTY

(1644–1912 A.D.)

In 1644 the Chinese Empire was once more conquered by barbarians, the Manchu Tartars. The Ch'ing dynasty produced two rulers of supreme quality, the Emperor K'ang Hsi (1662–1722 A.D.) and the Emperor Ch'ien Lung (1736–1795 A.D.). During the long period of their two reigns China passed through a period of such prosperity that it is hardly surprising that the applied arts should have reached an extremely high, if somewhat academic, standard. In particular the potters achieved technically and often artistically a level which has never been surpassed.

K'ANG HSI CERAMICS 'FAMILLE VERTE' ETC.

Their methods were essentially those of the Ming dynasty, and it is in refinement of shape and a more brilliantly successful quality of glaze and enamel that their supremacy is acknowledged. A few self-colour glazes of new type, notably the celebrated *lang yao* sang-de-bœuf and apple-green were invented, while the introduction of a blue enamel in place of the underglaze blue of the Ming five-colour and a rose-coloured enamel, derived from gold, mark innovations in the overglaze type of decoration. Porcelain in the reign of K'ang Hsi is chiefly notable for the group with overglaze enamel decoration of rich colours in which green predominates, known as 'famille verte'. A brilliant galaxy of green, yellow, aubergine, blue, rouge de fer, black and gold was used, sometimes on the biscuit, more often on a white glazed ground of surpassing purity. In the most splendid examples a background of black washed over with green (Pl. 131b), of yellow or of green was sometimes used; the first two of these, known respectively as 'famille noire' and 'famille jaune' were almost invariably executed on the biscuit. The taste of the decorator of the 'famille verte' varies considerably, sometimes painting a single exquisite figure against a plain ground (Pl. 129), at other times almost covering the surface of the piece with a luxuriant riot of elaborate motives (Pl. 128). But the design is always controlled, the execution invariably brilliantly planned with the colour-scheme contrastingly arranged. An adjunct often employed with panels of famille-verte decoration is the glaze of deep blue, blown on with a granular effect, which was one of the most successful inventions of the K'ang Hsi potter. This colour, known as powder blue, is often used in combination with gilt decoration and also with panels of underglaze blue and copper-red in reserve.

Ch'ing Dynasty

BLUE AND WHITE

The blue and white of the reign attains a brilliance which is unsurpassed (*Pl.* 130). The cobalt itself was subjected to the most rigorous processes of purification and with the resultant material the potter was able to produce the most surprising results, one of the most celebrated designs being the so-called 'hawthorn pattern' with sprays of prunus against a ground of cracked ice. The use of steatitic clay produced a crackled ground of a soft creamy tone, usually known as 'soft paste'. The combination of underglaze blue with celadon and copper-red produced one of the happiest results of the K'ang Hsi period.

SELF-COLOUR

The single-colour glazes include the well-known *lang yao* sang-de-bœuf, a brilliant crackled blood-red, the glaze under the base a translucent crystalline green; mirror-black, a deep glossy sepia, often enriched with gilding; and apple-green, a transparent green glaze washed over a greyish crackled glaze.

'FAMILLE ROSE'

Towards the close of the reign of K'ang Hsi and during that of his successors Yung Chēng (1723–1735 A.D.) and Ch'ien Lung (1736–1795 A.D.) a remarkable innovation appeared, the use of opaque enamels in varying shades in which pink predominates, known as a type as 'famille rose' (*Pl.* 139b). The palette is extremely delicate, consisting of pale green, yellows, blues, lilac, in all shades, with black, gold and iron-red to vary it. The general style of decoration is very well suited to the fragile porcelain on which it was used, much of which is of the type known in China as *t'o t'ai* (bodiless), in Europe as 'egg-shell'. A well-known group of plates with elaborate multiple borders, their backs coated with ruby enamel mark the highest point in this group, though almost equally lovely is the family with delicate painting of the style known as Ku yüeh hsüan (*Pl.* 138b). The name is often assumed to be that of a painter; it has also sometimes been said to be a Palace mark, the words meaning the Ku yüeh pavilion, but no such pavilion exists, and as the characters actually occur only on a few small glass vases, it is much more likely that they represent the name of the man they were made for or of the workshop which made them. With the trade with the West a number of types of European decoration were made for export, while for China itself the taste for European things, so popular among the Mandarins of the mid-eighteenth century, produced numberless objects with decoration copied in the main from European engravings.

Ch'ing Dynasty

The self-colour glazes of the latter part of the century are very various. The single red colour of the sang-de-bœuf becomes splashed and freckled with blue and purple, producing the type known as flambé. New shades of opaque single-colours such as coral, strawberry-red and clair-de-lune were much used, while the talents of the workmen were turned to such ingenious, but misguided, productions as the imitation of other materials, cloisonné, bronze or basket-work. The highly prized imperial wares of the Sung dynasty were also copied, many of them extremely successfully.

BLANC-DE-CHINE

At the factory of Tē-hua in the province of Fukien there was made from quite early on in the Ming dynasty a white porcelain with a beautiful creamy body and glaze; the greatest period of its output was at the end of the seventeenth and the beginning of the eighteenth century (*Pl.* 134*b*). The many figures of Kuan-yin, goddess of Mercy, are often marked by a liveliness of modelling and great charm of material, while the lovely little altar-cups and small bowls show that in domestic articles this factory was equally skilful.

STONEWARE

Another extensive group, many of which belong to a much earlier date, but the majority of which are to be placed in the eighteenth century, is the type of stoneware with heavily-splashed glazes made in Canton (Kuangtung) (*Pl.* 132). With them must be classed the red stoneware tea-pots, etc., made at I hsing, known in Europe as 'boccaro', the exportation of which influenced Böttger at Meissen and the brothers Elers in Staffordshire.

CH'ING PAINTING

In painting the period does not show much that was new. At the same time it is by no means lacking in masters of first-rate quality, and the Chinese themselves do not regard it as a period of decadence. On the contrary, the Southern School, in which they are most interested, produced in the seventeenth century the greatest masters of the Literary style in the 'Four Wangs'. These four masters, who are only artistically related, are thus called from having the first character of their names 'Wang' in common. They are Wang Shih-min, Wang Chien, Wang Hui and Wang Yüan-ch'i. According to Mr Waley, the third of those, Wang Hui (1632–1717), has the greatest reputation in China; but in some circles at least the last, Wang Yüan-ch'i (1642–1715), is preferred. A good example of his work is reproduced here (*Pl.* 122). These artists were honoured by the Emperor K'ang Hsi, who summoned them to his court and asked them to undertake literary as well as artistic work for him. Though equally conservative in their ideas they were much stronger in execution than the Ming exponents of this style. Being confident they were freer in touch and could indulge in subtleties without losing strength. During this time a new sort of technique was introduced, known as 'boneless' painting, consisting entirely in wash without the use of any line. This was practised by Wang Hui, and also by Chu Ta (*Pl.* 120). He set himself to conceal his skill behind the apparent carelessness of his execution. The last of the Literary painters whom we need mention is Yün Shou-p'ing or Nan-tien (1633–90), who did for flower-painting what the Four Wangs did for landscape. He was literary in his tastes and a conservative painter. Disliking the Ming tendency to impressionist flower-painting he returned to the realist art of Sung for his inspiration.

All these artists modelled their styles on the classic masters of Sung and Yüan. There were, however, a few artists working in newer styles. At the very beginning of the period Ch'ēn Hung-shou (1599–1652) seems to be showing the way for the development of a baroque school out of the mannerist painting of the day (*Pl.* 119). Others were experimenting in medium and using either a hot stylus or the finger-tip. There was also a return into favour of such hunting subjects as had delighted the Mongol conquerors in the Yüan period. One of the most successful artists who catered for this taste at the Manchu court was an Italian Jesuit, Giuseppe Castiglione, who worked for the Emperors Yung Chēng and Ch'ien Lung and received the Chinese name of Lang Shih-ning. He was extremely skilful in combining the science of European perspective and chiaroscuro with the technique of Chinese painting on silk. Such a painting by him as that from which a detail is here reproduced (*Pl.* 123) provides an interesting complement to the contemporary European taste for *chinoiserie*.

ENAMELS

In other arts the eighteenth century was singularly prolific. Cloisonné follows much the same lines as its Ming predecessors, though the designs tend to a close niggling form, nothing like so successful as the spacious planning of the Ming craftsman. At Canton was made the well-known enamel on a copper ground, known to the Chinese as *yang tz'u* or foreign porcelain, a product in the European style of Battersea or Bilston with delicate designs of 'famille rose' type painted on a white or coloured ground (*Pl.* 139a). The best pieces may be distinguished by their weight and by their extraordinarily finished painting, many of the finest having European subjects. To the eighteenth century also belong the majority of the carvings in ivory, a craft at which the Chinese have always excelled (*Pl.* 134*a*). Very few early pieces exist; a few are probably Ming and one at least, the relief of a yak (*Pl.* 93) in the Stoclet Collection at Brussels, may well be earlier. But most of the charming figures of Kuan-yin or Ho hsien ku, with their graceful lines following the curve of the tusk, belong to the seventeenth or eighteenth century, the best of them being probably products of the Palace workshops, established under K'ang Hsi. With them may be grouped the carvings in rhinoceros horn, a material thought in addition to its medicinal properties to have had the power, like the celadon dishes, of detecting poison. The semi-translucent dark brown horn lends itself to the making of small objects and a few of the altar-cups show real taste in the use of an uncommon substance.

TEXTILES

In silk weavings, in carpet-knotting and in velvets the Ch'ing workers were as skilful as their predecessors. The rich floral designs had a recognizable influence on contemporary European design; for they were much exported, while the wall-papers of elaborate description were made exclusively for the European market. Among the most remarkable of these weavings were the specially designed robes for the Emperor and his court with particular sets of ornament, used exclusively by one or other rank (*Pl.* 142). It is to the eighteenth century and later that largely belong the extensive group of fine embroideries, known in China as *hsiu hua* (*Pl.* 144). These are often of exceptional quality, the stitches mainly employed being long and short, stem and satin and Chinese knots, with couching and laidwork where metal thread was much used. The silk shawl which is so widely known as Spanish started its career in China and was much exported from there in the early part of the nineteenth century.

LACQUER

Under the Emperor Ch'ien Lung the lacquer industry was exceedingly flourishing, particularly in the court workshops in Peking (*Pl.* 127). There is little to distinguish it in design from its Ming forebears, except for a tendency to be lighter in weight and for the designs to be unusually complicated, but Ch'ien Lung himself showed a more delicate taste in the small wine-cups and saucers in the shape of chrysanthemum flowers, executed in plain red lacquer, which he had made for his own use. A particularly brilliant type inlaid with mother of pearl on a black ground is known as lac burgauté.

Another type of lacquer of almost equal importance is the so-called 'Coromandel' lacquer largely imported into Europe in the seventeenth and eighteenth century as screens and as panels for use in the making of chests, etc. (*Pl.* 126). These panels were executed in hard red wood, lacquered over with black with elaborate scenes cut away and coloured in bright pigments of a lac medium, the effect being brilliant in the extreme. Some of these panels and screens have been attributed to the Ming dynasty and a few doubtless belong to that period, but the majority of the better pieces do not probably date further back than the reign of K'ang Hsi (1662–1722 A.D.).

GLASS

Among the many workshops this Emperor set up in the palace was a glass shop. The history of glass, though a long one, can be illustrated by such few examples of an earlier date than the Ch'ing dynasty that it is hardly necessary to consider the family before that period. Known in China as *liu li* the glass output was almost exclusively coloured, either rich dark transparent blues, greens and reds or heavy opaque light colourings, such as turquoise, rose-pink or yellow (*Pl.* 138*a*). The date marks are often inscribed under the base in the manner of porcelain. The methods of the West such as blowing, moulding and pressing were all used, but it is in the carving of glass, in particular that type in which a deep colour on the surface is carved through to a lighter, that the most characteristic effects of Chinese glass are obtained.

JADE

It is this type of heavily carved decoration which also appears in many of the Ch'ing hardstone carvings, some of which are extremely beautiful. The soft qualities of the 'mutton fat' jade (*Pl.* 137), the moss-like surface of the dark-green jade (*Pl.* 136), the brilliant translucence of the emerald jadeite are treated with a great sense of material, even if the inspiration seems often tortuous and over-elaborated. It is the appreciation of the veinings and striations of stone that is an instinctive Chinese taste, which enables them so often to produce some surprising effect from an unpromising piece of material, an appreciation which also leads them to prize some curious natural formation of rock and treat it as an object of art.

NINETEENTH CENTURY

While in painting the academic tradition still persisted with, in some cases, very creditable results, in other respects the artistic output of China in the nineteenth century was extremely limited. The familiar carved ivory balls, the sets of chessmen, the fragile tortoiseshell and painted fans, the sandalwood boxes that our sea-faring ancestors brought home with such pride are the product of the Cantonese workshops. But they show ingenuity rather than aesthetic merit, nor did the potters, metal-workers, and weavers bring the level any higher. The great period of Chinese art really died with the Emperor Ch'ien Lung, and while there are reasons to hope that a revival of crafts may be taking place at the present day, it must be confessed that it is really in such things as the common *Tzŭ chou* rice bowl of the Peking coolie or the distinctive embroideries of the Yunnan peasantry that any trace of the great taste of the past survives.

II9. LADY AND GOD OF LONGEVITY
By Ch'ēn Hung-shou (*b. 1599; d. 1652*)

Painting in ink and light colours on paper
Size : 6' 4" × 3' 5"

BRITISH MUSEUM (FRAU OLGA WEGENER COLLECTION)

The painting is signed in full on the right side. 'Painted by Lao-lien Hung-shou of Ch'i-shan'. If genuine, it would be an important example of the work of this extremely individual artist who was one of the founders of the literary style. He showed a precocious mastery of painting and was never afraid of large compositions. Later he became a scholar and also came to court as Chamberlain to Ch'ung Chēng, the last Emperor of the Ming dynasty (1628–44). He was captured by the invading armies of the Manchus and survived till 1652, but he is a Ming artist. It is said of Ch'ēn Hung-shou's figure painting, 'Hung-shou's human figures are of gigantic and craggy stature; his draperies sharply moulded'. He also painted rocks and plants, and a number of compositions of this sort are in the Peking Palace collection. This somewhat *baroque* artist is quite individual and stands out among the painting of his day. He is perhaps a painter's painter.

Not previously published.

120. NARCISSUS
By CHU TA (*c. 1650*)

Ink on paper
Size: 12·125″ × 10·5″

BRITISH MUSEUM

Chu Ta was a member of the Ming Imperial family. Consequently, when the country fell to the Manchus in 1644 he became a priest and withdrew to live in solitude in the mountains. Stories are told of his wild and abandoned behaviour. He only painted when he chose and always made rapid sketches, hardly taking the brush from the paper. His signature betrays the same disregard of convention. He is best known by his literary name Pa-ta Shan-jēn and his fame in China has led to his work being much copied and forged. The present seems an undoubted example. In strength and freedom combined it would be hard to surpass it.

Not previously published.

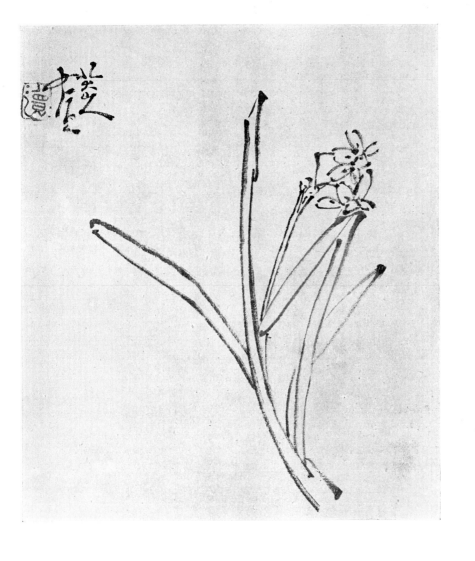

121. PHEASANTS AND FLOWERING TREES
By WANG WU. *Dated 1662*

Ink and full colours on silk
Size: 5' 6" × 3' 3"

BRITISH MUSEUM (EUMORFOPOULOS COLLECTION)

The painting is signed on the left 'K'ang Hsi Jēn Yin year (this is the first year of K'ang Hsi, 1662), spring month, painted by Wang Wu'. The artist Wang Wu or Wang-an was born in Soochow in 1632 and died in 1690. An account of him is given by Hirth (No. 21) who quotes Wang Shi-min in his praise on account of the 'spiritual expression of his paintings'. He seems to have specialized in flower painting. The imperial collection contained three paintings by him. This is a fine example of the mixed ink and colour paintings made by the early Ch'ing court artists.

Reference: Catalogue of the George Eumorfopoulos Collection, Chinese etc. Paintings, No. 50.

122. LANDSCAPE

By WANG YÜAN-CH'I (*b. 1642 ; d. 1715*)

Ink on paper
Size : 29·75″ × 21·5″

BRITISH MUSEUM (EUMORFOPOULOS COLLECTION)

Inscribed 'After Huang Ta-ch'ih's picture of Mount Fu-Ch'u by Wang Yüan-ch'i'.

Wang Yüan-ch'i is the fourth of the 'Four Wangs' who cultivated the literary landscape in ink during the hundred years from 1630 to 1730. They had a great respect for antiquity and particularly admired the great Yüan masters such as Chao Meng-fu, Wēn-chu, Ni T'san and (as here) Huang Kung-wang. They were patronized by the court and Wang Yüan-ch'i became an official of the Academy of Painting. In 1705 through the personal interest of K'ang Hsi he was appointed to superintend the compilation of *Shu Hua P'u*, an encyclopaedic history of calligraphy and painting. The present is an important example of his work and a very good example of the literary painting with its enormous range of ink tone and brush stroke.

References : Catalogue of the George Eumorfopoulos Collection, Chinese etc. Paintings No. 55. Chinese Paintings in English Collections, pl. liv.

123. THE HUNDRED HORSES IN PASTURE
By LANG SHIH-NING

(Giuseppe Castiglione: b. 1688; d. 1766)
Long scroll painting in colours on silk. Dated sixth year of Yung
Chēng (=1728)
Size: 24' 2" × 2' 9"
Detail: 2' 9" × 1' 10"

PALACE MUSEUM, PEKING

Giuseppe Castiglione was born at Milan in 1688. He arrived in China in August 1715 and in Peking in November of the same year, as a member of the mission of the Society of Jesus established there by the Portuguese. His skill in painting was such that he won high favour at the court from Yung Chēng and Ch'ien Lung. He became well known under his Chinese name of Lang Shih-ning and was able to be of service on a number of occasions to his fellow religionists in saving them from the persecutions of the Emperor. His style represents a true blend of Eastern and Western. Fifty-six of his paintings were recorded in the catalogue of the Imperial collections. Technically, these were all in the Chinese style. No oil painting by him is known and most of the paintings that pass under his name in Europe are late works by different hands.

He painted portraits of men, horses and dogs: flower studies and pictures of birds. The present scroll painting seems to be one of the most important works by him surviving. He has conformed so far with Chinese habit as to paint, not only in name, but in fact, a picture of a hundred horses.

References: Paul Pelliot, *T'oung Pao*, vol. xx, pp. 186–9, 1920–21. Ishida Mikino-suke, *A Bibliographical Study of Lang Shih-ning* (in Japanese, with English summary): *Bijutsu Kenkyu*, No. x, 1932. *Lang Shih-ning* 5 vols. of plates with Chinese titles. 1932–5. Published by the Peking Palace Museum.

124. NING YÜ-CH'UAN IN THE RÔLE OF NING CH'I WITH HIS OX
By HUANG SHĒN. *Dated 1744*

Hanging picture. Ink with light colours on silk
Size : 128·2 cm. × 49·1 cm. (50·375″ × 19·375″)

BRITISH MUSEUM (WEGENER COLLECTION)

This painting is identified by an inscription (at the top on the right) by the painter, as a portrait of his school friend, Ning Yü-ch'uan, whom he had not seen for thirty years, in the guise of his remote ancestor, Ning Ch'i. This is a famous character in Chinese history. He was discovered by Huan, Duke of Ch'i (684–642 B.C.) as a poor waggoner and was promoted to be Minister.

Huang Shēn's inscription is followed by four poems by different hands.

Huang Shēn was a native of Fukien. Born about 1700, he is an important literary painter of the eighteenth century. Notes on his career are given by Hirth (No. 39).

Reference : Chinese Paintings in English Collections, pl. lvii.

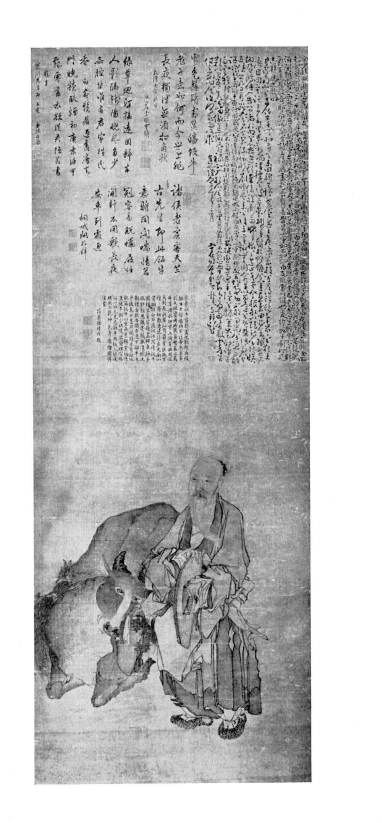

125. GIRL HOLDING A BIRD
By WANG CHAO-HSIANG (*18th century*)

Ink with touches of colour on paper
Size : 54″ × 24·5″

BRITISH MUSEUM (FRAU OLGA WEGENER COLLECTION)

A charming *genre* subject by an artist not otherwise known. We in
Europe are not accustomed to such slight work on so large a scale, but
the sure touch of the brushwork and clever use of small touches of
bright colour in the girdle, the shoes, and the berry that the girl is
offering the bird prevent any feeling of emptiness.

Not previously published.

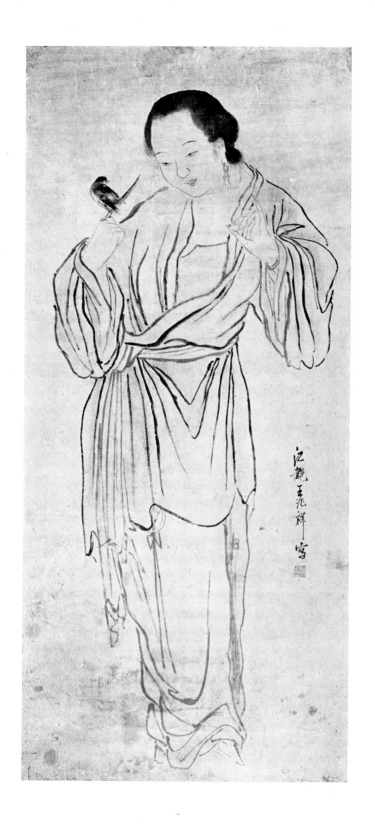

126. PANELS FROM A SCREEN
Period of K'ang Hsi (1662–1722 A.D.)

Incised lacquer : Height 8'

VICTORIA AND ALBERT MUSEUM, LONDON

Lacquer of this type, known in Europe as 'Coromandel', is made of wood lacquered a deep brown and incised with the required design, which is then coloured with lacquer pigments and gold leaf. The effect of these elaborate coloured designs against the dark ground is brilliant in the extreme. The majority of these screens belong to the eighteenth century, though some fine examples of the Ming dynasty are known.

127. IMPERIAL THRONE

Period of Ch'ien Lung (1736–1795 A.D.)

Cinnabar-red Peking lacquer : Height 42″

VICTORIA AND ALBERT MUSEUM, LONDON

This throne, which is said to have been used by Ch'ien Lung, was certainly intended by the motives of the decoration for Imperial use. It is a superb example of the type of lacquer executed in the eighteenth century by the Palace workshops.

Ch'ing Dynasty

128. VASE
Reign of K'ang Hsi (1662–1722 A.D.)

Porcelain : Height 17"

VICTORIA AND ALBERT MUSEUM, LONDON
(SALTING COLLECTION)

Painted with a design of prunus and birds on rocks in pale-green, yellow, aubergine and blue, with a few touches of iron-red, on a white ground. In a period when the tendency was to stress the strong in colour, this lovely vase with its restrained palette stands out as an example of the refinement which the Chinese could employ in an essentially decorative piece.

Ch'ing Dynasty

129. DISH
Reign of K'ang Hsi (1662–1722 A.D.)

Porcelain: Diameter 13·4"

VICTORIA AND ALBERT MUSEUM, LONDON
(SALTING COLLECTION)

Painted in coloured enamels of the 'famille verte' with a woman and a child in a garden. Of several hands or workrooms, which may be distinguished in K'ang Hsi porcelain decoration, none is more successful than the artist or shop which produced these large-figure designs with their admirable spacing, graceful poses and emphasis on the heavily-massed hair.

130. PLATE
Reign of K'ang Hsi (1662–1722 A.D.)

Porcelain : Diameter 10·75"

VICTORIA AND ALBERT MUSEUM, LONDON

Painted in underglaze blue of varying tones, the design of lotus-plants and storks is distinguished by the sensitive drawing which so often marks the lovely porcelain of this reign. The mind that designed the free and tremulous plants on the border was that of a master.

131*a*. DRAGON-HORSE (LUNG-MA)
Period of K'ang Hsi (1662–1722 A.D.)

Porcelain : Height 8″

DR VON KLEMPERER, BERLIN

Enamelled in green, yellow and aubergine over the biscuit, this animal belongs to a large group of livelily modelled birds and beasts, which were made, usually in pairs, for decorative purposes in the Ch'ing dynasty.

131*b*. SAUCER
Reign of K'ang Hsi (1662–1722 A.D.)

Porcelain : Diameter 5″

VICTORIA AND ALBERT MUSEUM, LONDON

An example of the celebrated 'famille noire' with decoration in enamels of the 'famille verte' against a ground of black washed over with green enamel.

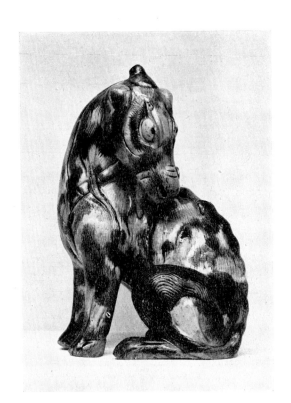

132. VASE

Kwangtung ware of the 18th century

Stoneware: Height 14"

VICTORIA AND ALBERT MUSEUM, LONDON

Covered with a soft bluish-white crackled glaze this piece belongs to a large class of stonewares made in the south of China at Yang Chiang. The glazes are almost always opalescent in tone and varying from white to purplish-blue. It is plain that these wares were made with glazes in imitation of those of Sung times, which, indeed, from their colouring is fairly obvious. They were known as 'the blue mottled glazes copying the Chün yao'.

cf. *Ching-tē Chēn T'ao lu* in S. Julien, *Histoire et Fabrication de la Porcelaine Chinoise*, 1856.

133a. WATER-POT
Mark and Reign of K'ang Hsi (1662–1722 A.D.)

Porcelain: Height 2·8"

VICTORIA AND ALBERT MUSEUM, LONDON

Decorated with clouds in slip under a celadon glaze, this little inkwell
is a masterpiece of the self-colours for which the K'ang Hsi potters were
as celebrated as for their brilliant enamelled products.

133b. BOWL
Period of Yung Chēng (1723–1735 A.D.)

Porcelain: Height 7"

MUSEUM OF FINE ARTS, BOSTON

Painted with bunches of grapes in underglaze copper-red on a *fouetté*
lavender ground.

134*a*. HO HSIEN KU
Probably 17th century

Ivory with traces of paint : Height 8"

M. ADOLPHE STOCLET, BRUSSELS

One of the Eight Immortals.

134*b*. WOMAN PLAYING A MUSICAL INSTRUMENT
About 1700

Blanc-de-chine : Height 7"

DR VON KLEMPERER, BERLIN

The white-glazed porcelain made at Fukien in the province of Te hua
was famous in Europe under the name of blanc-de-chine. Its export to
the West was considerable from the end of the seventeenth century
onwards, but a number of marked pieces of earlier date are known, and
it is likely that some of these pieces go back to the Yüan dynasty or even
earlier.

Reference : Berlin Exhibition Catalogue, No. 999.

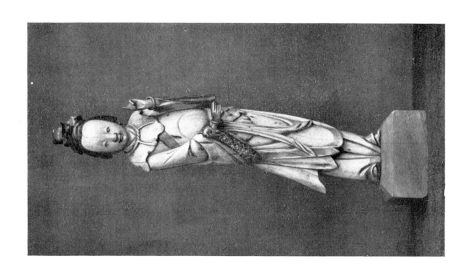

135. PILGRIM BOTTLE
Mark and Reign of Ch'ien Lung (1736–1795 A.D.)

Porcelain : Height 10″

MR R. BRUCE, LONDON

Painted in blue, pale green and rose-pink enamels.

136. TABLE-SCREEN
Period of Ch'ien Lung (1736–1795 A.D.)

Dark green jade : Height 13″

MR R. BRUCE, LONDON

From the Summer Palace, Peking.

137. BRUSH-POT
Period of Ch'ien Lung (1736–1795 A.D.)

Translucent white jade : Height 8″

MR R. BRUCE, LONDON

From the Summer Palace, Peking.

Ch'ing Dynasty

138a. BOTTLE
Period of Ch'ien Lung (1736–1795 A.D.)

Glass: Height 6″

VICTORIA AND ALBERT MUSEUM, LONDON
(SALTING COLLECTION)

A typical example of eighteenth century glass with flowers cut away
from a layer of pink through to a ground of turquoise.

138b. BOTTLE
Period of Ch'ien Lung (1736–1795 A.D.)

Porcelain: Height 3·55″

SIR PERCIVAL DAVID, LONDON

Enamelled in 'famille rose' colours in the delicate style known as Ku-
yüeh-hsüan (cf. p. 302).

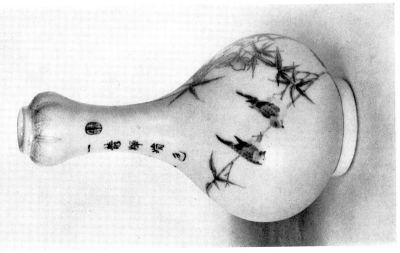

139*a*. DISH

Period of Ch'ien Lung (1736–1795 A.D.)

Enamel on Copper : Width 12"

VICTORIA AND ALBERT MUSEUM, LONDON

An example of the fine enamelled ware made at Canton in the eighteenth century. The subject, derived no doubt from a European print, is an example of the *Goût Européen* which we know had a vogue at the Chinese court very similar to the taste for Far Eastern things prevalent in Europe.

139*b*. SAUCER DISH

Reign of Yung Chēng (1723–1735 A.D.)

Porcelain : Diameter 7·8"

VICTORIA AND ALBERT MUSEUM, LONDON
(SALTING COLLECTION)

An example of the highest quality of *famille rose* enamelling. The back of the plate is covered with a ruby enamel, as in so many of the finest pieces.

140. DISH

Mark and Reign of Yung Chēng (1723–1735 A.D.)

Porcelain : Diameter 19·8″

VICTORIA AND ALBERT MUSEUM, LONDON

This dish, painted in enamels of the *famille rose,* with its well-spaced design and flickering brushwork, is a perfect example of the exquisite quality in drawing and colouring, so characteristic of the refined taste of the Yung Chēng period.

141. CARPET
18th century

Wool : Length 7′

VICTORIA AND ALBERT MUSEUM, LONDON

Knotted in shades of blue and brown, the main field white.

142. IMPERIAL ROBE
18th century

Embroidered silk: Height 4' 5·2"

VICTORIA AND ALBERT MUSEUM, LONDON

Embroidered with coloured silks and metal thread on a yellow ground and lined with grey squirrel and ermine. Five-clawed dragons, facing to the front (for the use of the Emperor only, when on the shoulders in addition to the body), the eight Buddhist felicitous emblems and Mt Meru, sacred to all Buddhists, rising from the sea. Satin, stem and split stitches, couched work.

143. PANEL
17–18th century

Silk tapestry (k'o ssŭ) : Height 21"

MR WRIGHT LUDINGTON, SANTA BARBARA, CALIFORNIA

An exquisite example of the fineness of technique of which the Chinese
tapestry weavers were capable.

144. MARRIAGE-BED CURTAIN
18th century

Embroidered silk damask : Height 52"

Embroidered with mandarin ducks, herons and water-plants in two shades of blue on a crimson silk damask; mainly satin stitch.

SELECT BIBLIOGRAPHY

GENERAL

Kokka Magazine. 1889–1935.

S. W. Bushell. *Chinese Art.* 2 vols. 1904–06.

O. Muensterberg. *Chinesische Kunstgeschichte.* 2 vols. 1910.

E. F. Fenollosa. *Epochs of Chinese and Japanese Art.* 2 vols. 1912.

T'oung Pao. 1912–1935.

J. C. Ferguson. *Outlines of Chinese Art.* 1919.

Burlington Magazine. Monograph on Chinese Art. 1925.

O. Siren. *History of Early Chinese Art.* 4 vols. 1929–30.

M. Rostovtzev. *Animal Style in S. Russia and China.* 1929.

O. Kümmel. *Chinesische Kunst.* 1930.

O. Kümmel. *Jörg Trübner zum Gedächtnis.* 1930.

R. Koechlin. *Souvenirs d'un Vieil Amateur d'Art de l'Extrême-Orient.* 1930.

G. Soulié de Morant. *History of Chinese Art.* 1931.

D. Goldschmidt. *L'Art Chinois.* 1931.

EXHIBITIONS (Catalogues)

London. Burlington Fine Arts Club. *Chinese Pottery and Porcelain.* 1910.

Paris. *Exposition à la Rue de la Ville l'Evesque.* 1913.

New York. Metropolitan Museum. *Early Chinese Pottery.* 1916.

Hague. *Société des Amis de l'Art Asiatique,* 1925.

Tokyo. *Exhibition of Famous Chinese Paintings (Toso Gemmin Meigwa Taikan).* 1929.

Berlin. *Ausstellung Chinesischer Kunst.* 1929.

Paris. *Exposition des Bronzes Chinois au Musée du Louvre.* 1933.

PAINTING

Shimbi Taikwan. *Selected Relics of Japanese and Chinese Art.* Kyoto. 1899–1908.

F. Hirth. *Scraps from a Collector's Notebook, being Some Notes on Chinese Painters of the Present Dynasty.* Leyden, 1905.

Toyo Bijutsu Taikwan. *Masterpieces selected from the Fine Arts of the Far East.* Vols. viii–x. Tokyo, 1909–10.

L. Binyon. *Painting in the Far East.* 1st ed. 1908; 4th ed. 1934.

R. Petrucci. *La Philosophie de la Nature dans l'Art d'Extrême-Orient.* Paris, 1910.

H. A. Giles. *An Introduction to the History of Chinese Pictorial Art.* 2nd ed. 1918.

P. Pelliot. *Les Grottes de Touen-Houang.* 6 vols. 1920–24.

Bibliography

A. Stein. *The Thousand Buddhas*. 1921.

A. Waley. *An Index of Chinese Artists represented in the British Museum*. 1922.

A. Waley. *An Introduction to the Study of Chinese Painting*. 1923.

L. Binyon. *Chinese Paintings in English Collections*. Paris, 1927.

O. Siren. *Chinese Paintings in American Collections*. 5 pts. Paris, 1927–28.

A. Waley. *Catalogue of Paintings recovered from Tun-huang by Sir Aurel Stein*. 1931.

O. Fischer. *Die Chinesische Malerei der Han-Dynastie*. 1931.

O. Siren. *A History of Early Chinese Painting*. 2 vols. 1933.

Ku Kung Hua Shu Chi (Peiping Palace Museum, Paintings and Calligraphy). 45 pts. 1930–36.

K. Tomita. *Portfolio of Chinese Paintings in the Boston Museum (Han to Sung periods)*. 1933.

SCULPTURE

E. Chavannes. *Mission Archéologique dans la Chine Septentrionale*. 3 vols. 1913–15.

L. Ashton. *Introduction to the Study of Chinese Sculpture*. 1924.

A. Salmony. *Chinesische Plastik*. 1925.

V. Segalen, G. de Voisins and J. Lartigue. *Mission Archéologique en Chine*. 1923.

O. Siren. *Chinese Sculpture*. 4 vols. 1925.

S. Omura. *Chinese Sculpture*. (Shina bijutsu-shi). 1915.

ICONOGRAPHY

W. P. Yetts. *Catalogue of the Eumorfopoulos Collection*. vol. 3. Buddhist Sculpture. 1932.

BRONZES

Hsi ch'ing ku chien (1749). Facsimile of Ch'ien lung's Catalogue. 1888.

T'ao chai chi chin lu (Tuan Fang Collection). 1908.

E. A. Voretzsch. *Altchinesischen Bronzen*. 1924.

W. P. Yetts. *Chinese Bronzes*. 1925.

Sumitomo Collection of Bronzes. *Catalogue*. 1921–26.

W. P. Yetts. *Eumorfopoulos Collection. Catalogue of the Chinese and Corean Bronzes* (etc.). 2 vols. 1929–30.

Stockholm. *Ostasiatiska Samlingarna. Exhibition Catalogue*. 1933.

W. C. White. *Tombs of Old Lo-yang*. 1934.

JADES

E. Biot. *Le Tcheou-li*. 1851.

Wu T'a ch'êng. *Ku yü t'u k'ao*. 1889.

Bibliography

Bishop Collection of Jade. *Metropolitan Museum Handbook, No. 10.*
B. Laufer. *Jade.* 1912.
U. Pope-Hennessy. *Early Chinese Jades.* 1923.
P. Pelliot. *Jades Archaïques.* 1925.

CERAMICS

S. W. Bushell. *T'ao shuo.* 1910.
R. L. Hobson. *Chinese Pottery and Porcelain.* 2 vols. 1915.
A. L. Hetherington. *Early Ceramic Wares of China.* 1922.
O. Rücker-Embden. *Chinesische Frühkeramik.* 1922.
R. L. Hobson. *Wares of the Ming Dynasty.* 1923.
R. L. Hobson. *Handbook to the Pottery and Porcelain of the Far East. British Museum,* 1937.
E. Zimmermann. *Chinesische Porzellan,* 1923.
R. L. Hobson. *Catalogue of the Eumorfopoulos Collection.* Vols. 1–6. 1925–28.
R. L. Hobson. *Later Ceramic Wares of China.* 1925.
W. B. Honey. *Guide to the later Chinese Porcelain. Victoria and Albert Museum.* 1927.
R. L. Hobson. *Catalogue of the Leonard Gow Collection.* 1931.
Hsiang Yüan-pien. Edited by Kuo Pao-chiang and J. C. Ferguson. 1931.
R. L. Hobson. *Catalogue of Chinese Pottery and Porcelain in the Collection of Sir P. David.* 1934.
L. Reidemeister. *Ming-Porzellane in Schwedischen Sammlungen.* 1935.

TEXTILES

O. Von Falke. *Kunstgeschichte der Seidenweberei.* 2 vols. 1913.
F. H. Andrews. *Ancient Chinese Figured Silks.* 1920.
Kendrick. *Catalogue of Mohammedan Textiles of the Mediaeval Period. Victoria and Albert Museum.* 1924.
Victoria and Albert Museum. *Brief Guide to the Chinese Woven Fabrics.*
Victoria and Albert Museum. *Brief Guide to the Chinese Embroideries.*
New York Metropolitan Museum. *Chinese Textiles* (Priest and Simmons).
A. F. Kendrick and C. E. C. Tattersall. *Handwoven Carpets.* 2 vols. 1922.
W. P. Yetts. *Discoveries of the Kozlov Expedition. Burlington Magazine,* April, 1926.

ARCHITECTURE

E. Boerschmann. *Die Baukunst und religiöse Kultur der Chinesen.* 3 vols. 1911–31.
O. Siren. *Walls and Gates of Pekin.* 1924.

INDEX

Index

Index